CITIZENS *for* EISENHOWER

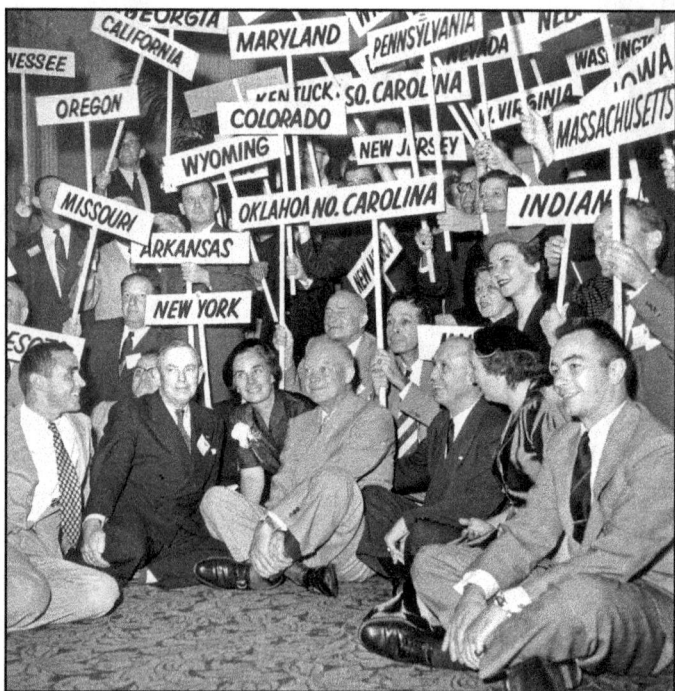

Ike and some of the "Citizens" team at the 1952 Republican Presidential Nominating Convention. At left, Charlie Willis; at right, Stan Rumbough; center, Ike, flanked by Citizens Co-Chairmen Mary Lord, left, and Walter Williams, right.   [Photo: Bettie Zacher]

CITIZENS *for* EISENHOWER

Stanley M. Rumbough, Jr.

International Publishers / McLean, VA

Copyright © 2013, International Publihsers
1350 Beverly Rd., Suite 617, McLean, VA 22101-3922
(703) 397-9600 / customersvc@internationalpublishers.us

ISBN-13: 978-0615863559
ISBN-10: 0615863558

Library of Congress Control Number: 2013947954

For my lovely former wife Nedenia—better known as **Dina Merrill**—the mother of my children, who was always supportive of my efforts with "Citizens" and at the White House. She postponed her dream career to raise our family in New York City and Washington; when I went back to my own business, she went on to grand success with her true love, acting.

And, with thanks to: **George A. Colburn**, Executive Producer, the Eisenhower Legacy Project, for his thoughtful review and helpful suggestions, Brigadier General **Carl Reddel** (USAF, Ret.), Executive Director of the Eisenhower Memorial Commission, for his support and assistance, and Deputy Director **Timothy Rives** and the Staff at the Eisenhower Presidential Library (Abilene KS), **Christopher Abraham, Kevin Bailey**, and **Chalsea Milner.**

And last . . . but certainly not least, I salute our editor, **Brayton Harris**, who assisted with my research, teased forth memories long buried, and kept us on target . . . and on schedule,

LIST OF ILLUSTRATIONS

CONTENTS

1945: A pair of ex-fighter pilots—one Navy, one Marine Corps, start a successful airline—and lose it three years later, thanks to some questionable government rulings in favor of a less-successful competitor. Who, soon enough, went out of business.

Frustrated with "the government," they seek a change and build an "Eisenhower for President" network, with—after eight months—more than 800 active Clubs in 38 states providing advice, assistance, resources, and discipline for disciples.

A bit of history: earlier efforts by others, beginning in 1943, aimed at an Eisenhower presidency . . . including President Truman, who saw Ike as a winner for the Democrats.

Efforts . . . in the Fall of 1951 . . . everyone is trying to make a "candidate" out of the general . . . including, briefly, again, President Truman. The "official" Eisenhower for President committee is formed by long-time supporters and professional politicians. They do not, at this point, have any connection with the two former fighter pilots.

The co-founders of the "Eisenhower for President Clubs" are about out of money; they get some good advice: create a formal organization ("Citizens for Eisenhower") with professional management and fundraising help. Done.

EDITOR'S NOTE

The story of "Citizens for Eisenhower" has been told to some degree—notably, in two chapters of Jane Dick's 1980 book, *Volunteers and the Making of Presidents*, and in a few pages of Eisenhower's 1963 memoir *Mandate for Change*—but with so little detail that few books that cover any aspects of the election of 1952 mention "Citizens" if at all, and those that do, generally get it all wrong.

And yet—as Eisenhower himself acknowledged and much to the irritation of professional politicians—"Citizens" played a key role in persuading him to run for president, in the first place. In June, 1951, Charles F. Willis, Jr. and Stanley M. Rumbough. Jr.—two entrepreneurial WWII fighter-pilots with no political experience but with a great deal of enthusiasm and idealistic to the core—took the first steps toward "Citizens" because they were frustrated with what they saw as "that mess" in Washington and just knew, instinctively, that General of the Army Dwight D. Eisenhower could not only win election but would bring rational order to endemic chaos. Charlie and Stan had never communicated with the general and were so naive that they didn't even know how candidates were nominated.

But they made it work.

So . . . to begin with, who were these two young guys, barely in their thirties . . . where did they come from, what had they learned along the way, and how did they help create the most successful "draft" political movement, to that time, of the 20th Century? And what lessons can we pass on to future dreamers? Stanley Rumbough tells their story.

Read on . . .

Brayton Harris

INTRODUCTION

Let me set my stage, so to speak. Before there was any formal "Eisenhower for President" movement, it was just my partner Charlie Willis, me, our first volunteer (Dolly Hirshon), and a plan. We would create so much public demand for Ike to run, that he would have to say "Yes." We started building "Eisenhower Clubs" one state at a time, and within eight months, our organization included thousands of volunteers working out of our headquarters and more than 800 "Eisenhower Clubs" spread over 38 states. By that point, I must acknowledge, we were no longer alone. Myriad other Eisenhower fans and professional politicians were pursuing the same goal . . . and Ike said, "Yes."

Our mission, you might say, was over. Well, no. We set another goal: help Ike get the Republican nomination, and we mobilized our forces to sway voters in the states that held primary elections, to charm convention delegates in the others, and to overwhelm attendees at the Chicago nominating convention with hype and hoopla. Ike won.

And then . . . the campaign. By this time, "Citizens for Eisenhower" included more than a million volunteers from all political parties or none at all, who wanted to see Ike in the White House. We held rallies for Ike, mobilized crowds for speeches, and participated in the development and sponsorship of the first-ever political spots on television. And we worked a classic get-out-the-vote plan, from manning phone banks to remind, to taking people to the polls to vote. Ike won.

This is a memoir, but includes information that comes from outside my memory, and some that is outside my direct experience but is relevant to the topic at hand. My personal staff and I have combed through my files, contemporary newspapers and magazines, memoirs and biographies by or about other participants, more recent scholarly reviews and studies, and, of most import, the archives at the Eisenhower Presidential Library in Abilene, Kansas.

From all, I have assembled bits and pieces of our overall story—some vital, some merely interesting, which have never been put together in a coherent narrative. Please understand: "ours" is not a comprehensive history of the Presidential Campaign of 1952. We were supporting, not driving, the campaign, but I do believe, we made a difference.

Many stories to be told, many lessons-learned and suggestions to be passed along for future campaigns.

But let me start, at the beginning, more or less. How I got involved, in the first place.

Stanley Rumbough, Jr.
Palm Beach, FL, August 2013

CHAPTER ONE

Right after the attack on Pearl Harbor, December 7, 1941, I signed up for Navy flight school. The training command was overwhelmed with applicants, and the recruiter told me to go on back to college—I was a senior at Yale—and graduate, and there would be a slot waiting for me.

My family thought my choice of service was a bit odd . . . my father, grandfather, and great-grandfather Rumbough were all West Pointers, Army all the way. And my father, Stanley Maddox Rumbough Sr., was named after his maternal grandfather (General David Stanley, West Point, Class of 1852). His middle name (Maddox) was chosen in honor of the officer who was slated to be best-man at his parent's wedding but who had been killed in an Indian ambush on the way to the ceremony.

However, I didn't want to trade on heritage and "connections." Many of my father's classmates (1909) were now general officers, and had I joined the Army, I just knew that I would likely be routed off to some cushy job as a general's aide. I wanted to be a pilot. This was not a casual bit of youthful bravado; I already had a civilian pilot's license.

My Navy training started in May with pre-flight

ground school in Chapel Hill, North Carolina, followed by basic flight training at Grosse Ile, Michigan, then advanced training at Pensacola—at the end of which I was offered a chance to switch to the Marine Corps. I was taken by their motto, "A few good men," so, why not? By the end of December, 1943, after some more training at the Marine air base at El Toro, California, I was on my way for duty, far out into the Pacific. Where I was teamed up—in a manner of speaking—with perhaps the finest fighter aircraft of the war, the F-4U Corsair.

And then—if I may insert an instructive note—I met a true aviation icon, Charles Lindbergh. My squadron was engaged in the Marshall Islands campaign, early 1944, and Colonel Lindbergh, working as a civilian advisor for the company that designed and built the Corsair, had joined us for a time as a roving test pilot. Did we have any problems, were there things that could be improved? One example: the design load for "externals"—bombs—was 1000 pounds. Lindbergh showed us how to take it up to 3000 pounds, any time we did not have to fly above 10,000 feet . . . that is, any time we knew we would not have to be prepared for air-to-air combat. Two steps: one, take off with partial flaps (usually deployed only on landing) to increase lift, and two, open the cowl vents to prevent overheating. Brilliant, and it worked. And I learned a simple lesson: don't believe everything you read in the manual, take nothing for granted, always look around the corner to see if you might find a better way.

Fighter pilot Stanley M. Rumbough, Jr., U.S. Marine Corps, 1944

My combat tours were not nearly as exciting as those of some of my squadron mates, although I did come close enough to satisfy my need for adventure. On one mission, flying my Corsair out of a captured airstrip on Tarawa to bomb the island of Nauru, I was hit by anti-aircraft fire . . . and soon enough saw a steady-stream of oil tracking across my right wing.

Now, this mission was at the limit of our operational range and the Corsairs did not have very sophisticated navigation gear, so we had been escorted to the target by a P2V patrol plane. When I reported my problem, the P2V radioed back to Tarawa to send out a PBY flying boat to escort me home and, of course, to be prepared to make a water landing and rescue should I have to ditch—that is, make a controlled crash—into the ocean.

Well, three of my squadron mates had already tried ditching on other missions, and two of them did not survive. So it was steady-on, very conservative, no major changes in any control setting unless absolutely necessary.

I made it back to Tarawa. The oil capacity of a Corsair was 24 gallons. When I came to a stop on the runway . . . there was one pint remaining.

I met my partner in political persuasion—Charlie Willis—after the war, because Charlie's wife Grace ("Bo") had been the boarding-school roommate of the girl I would soon marry, Nedenia Hutton. Deenie had been a maid of honor at Bo's June 1945 wedding to Charlie (and Bo would be part of our March, 1946 wedding).

Well, let me set another stage. When I was a sophomore at Yale, Deenie was dating my roommate Francis (Frank) Trudeau. Her mother, Marjorie Merriweather Post, had a nice tradition: every spring, she would invite Deenie to bring some friends, male and female, for a Spring Break/Easter party at their grand Palm Beach estate (known then and now as Mar-a-Lago, although it's now owned by Donald Trump). Deenie would invite a few of her girl friends, and her current boyfriend would invite an equal number of young men. Of which, I was one. A couple of years later, Deenie had changed boyfriends—by a grand coincidence, to another of my roommates, Bertrand Taylor. And I enjoyed another Spring Break in Palm Beach.

Well, soon enough I was off to war and Deenie was off to a year at college and then to study at the American Academy of Dramatic Arts. In February, 1945, my combat tour had ended . . . I might note, in passing, that I was honored with two awards of the Distinguished Flying Cross and eight Air Medals, certification that I was earning my pay. Well, I had some leave time coming and returned to New York for a visit . . . where the only single girl I knew, was Deenie. So I called her; she invited me over for cocktails. It was a nice visit, so I asked, might she join me for dinner the next evening? And she said, that would be nice, except, under her new stage name, Dina Merrill, she was on her way to the middle of the Pacific—which I had just left—for a two-month tour as member of a USO troupe.

My leave was soon finished and the Marine Corps sent me back to school for training as a combat instrument flight instructor . . . but by August, the war had ended. They told me, go home, stay in touch by telephone, we'll let you know when your discharge has been processed. "Home" was New York; I began courting Deenie, and met her best friend—Bo Willis— and of course, Bo's husband Charlie; we became instant friends. By October, I was a civilian working for my father as director of sales at a very successful family business, the White Metal company—which made metal tubes.

At the same time, Charlie decided to start his own airline. Willis Air Service.

This was not such a crazy idea; Charlie was one of the most experienced American pilots in the war. He had joined the Navy in 1940 and "earned" his first of three Purple Hearts during the attack on Pearl Harbor. He went on to fly 250 missions in the Pacific and another 35 in Europe, variously flying patrol planes, bombers, and fighters. He had *his* share of adventures: on one mission, Charlie rescued an Army Air Forces general officer who had been shot down and managed to reach a small island in Japanese-held territory. On another, Charlie himself was shot down and spent four days bobbing around in a rubber life-raft. He was credited with helping sink a Japanese destroyer and a German submarine. Along the way, he was awarded three Distinguished Flying Crosses. Charlie, to say the least, was fearless. And focused. And he knew a lot about airplanes . . . what they could do, and not do, and how to tell the difference.

In truth, a number of airlines were started at the same time by ex-military pilots, flying bargain-base-ment war surplus planes, many on lease from the Army. Some of these start-ups went into passenger service, but a couple of dozen pioneered a new concept, mov-ing freight—not just packages—by air. That's more or less what they did, flying cargo in the war, and now they applied that experience to a civilian world that had never moved freight by air.

I admit, I was envious. Charlie was creating excitement while I was stuck in a job with, literally, nothing to do. Yes, as I noted, I was "director of sales" and the company was very successful . . . but, it was so successful that it had back-orders sufficient to keep the place going for a long time, at full capacity, and I had, literally, nothing to sell. So in December, I moved over to working with Charlie.

With a few military versions of the two-engine DC-3 and four-engine DC-4, Willis Air Service began operating out of a dirt-airstrip at the Teterboro (NJ) Airport. Our first office was a tent and our wives were the staff and the business was funded from savings (which were quite healthy; there had not been many opportunities to spend money in the middle of the war in the middle of the Pacific). We started operations with targets of opportunity, for example, flying the latest designer dresses from New York to Neiman-Marcus in Dallas, and taking unfinished textile goods—tablecloths, shirts, whatever, to Puerto Rico to be embellished with hand-embroidery. Gave us some practice, but not much business until we began flying charter flights between the U. S., South America and the Caribbean. Flowers, fruit and vegetables from grower to seller. Shrimp from New Orleans to anywhere; cattle from Texas to farmers in Columbia. Time sensitive cargoes, and reliability was key to our success.

And our success—the success of any of the new freight airlines—was key to some complaints soon filed with the Civil Aviation Board (CAB)—filed, that is, by the "major" airlines. Even though they rarely carried non-passenger cargo other than letter mail and parcel post, and even though some of their operation was subsidized by the government, we—not subsidized in any fashion—were accused of hurting their business! Among other things, they charged, we were operating a "scheduled" airline without a legally-required "certificate of public convenience and necessity." We told the CAB, "We do charters, which are allowed without a certificate. We're not 'scheduled,' we leave whenever the plane is loaded."

The CAB countered, "You fly every day. That's a schedule."

We said, "OK, give us a certificate."

They said, "Not so fast. We have to study this whole air-freight thing." We continued flying while they studied, and a full year later—May, 1947—they issued an interim ruling that would allow us and some other start-ups to operate over designated routes, on a regular schedule, flying cargo only, until such time as the matter had been more fully studied. As it happened, that would take another two years (yes, your Federal government at work), but we were at least given a temporary permit to operate on a specified route, up and down the East Coast.

And, operate we did. In addition to handling freight between the Northeast and Florida, we immediately began daily freight service to Puerto Rico; by the end of 1947, Willis Air Service accounted for 53 percent of *all* commercial air traffic in and out of the island. This was more traffic than the regular airlines that served the island—Pan American and Eastern— and all irregular carriers, combined. And suddenly, at the end of December, the CAB said, "Oh, we're not sure if Puerto Rico is included in your permit. We'll have to study the matter." And they ordered us to cease that operation . . . within 24 hours. We had cargo piled up and waiting at both ends, which we had to abandon, which, as you will understand, did not sit well with our customers. And oh, by the way, the CAB never gave us a final ruling. I am still waiting . . .

By this time—the end of 1947—we had long since moved out of the tent and into a new hangar, and had arranged—through a simple barter—to have the dirt airstrip paved by one of the major fuel suppliers, in exchange for exclusive gassing rights at Teterboro. We also leased a couple of small fully-equipped repair and overhaul shops.

Then, because we had the equipment and in-house trained staff—and wanted to keep all fully-occupied, call it, leveraging our assets—we expanded into pro- viding ground services . . . loading and un-loading, re- fueling, inspections and maintenance, repairs . . . for, among other clients, the Army Corps of Engineers, private aircraft owners, corporate flight departments, and two other freight-only airlines also operating out of Teterboro.

Our flight operations were steady, and we were building a strong customer base and I do believe that by 1948, Willis Air Service was one of the top five air freight carriers in the United States. Then, with the grateful approval, I am sure, of the regular scheduled airlines, the CAB decided it was time to thin out the herd, so to speak. Of some twenty-four companies that were operating on a "temporary" (by then, approaching two years) permit, they would certify only four.

Eastern Airlines, which served the same New York to Florida route on which we operated, argued before the CAB that no other air service was needed, they—Eastern—could handle the freight by themselves, thank you very much, and they didn't need the annoyance of "wasteful" competition from such upstarts as Willis which, Eastern told the CAB, was "not fit, willing, and able."

All of the applicants were given a thorough inspection by CAB examiners: they recommended that Willis Air Service be one of the four. The CAB ignored the recommendation. In 1949, our "route" was granted to United States Airlines (no relation to any airline with a similar name, then or now). We asked, "Why?" We were told, because we didn't have enough money in the bank, therefore, were not stable.

For the year 1948, our profit from flight operations was $24,881. U. S. Airlines had a loss of $313,488. (For the equivalent in today's money, multiply all dollar amounts by ten.) We had 3.5 times as many revenue ton-miles; our ton-mile expenses were only one-fifth as much as theirs. We had 192 employees; they had 60.

Which of us would you think was the most likely to succeed? Well, for reasons certainly unknown to me, they had clout, we had nothing and the CAB was deaf, dumb, and blind to our pleading. There weren't enough dresses moving between New York and anywhere to keep us afloat, and we had to close down.[1]

We had one remaining asset: along the way, based on our track record and contacts made at Teterboro, we had acquired the fueling contracts for Idyllwild—now JFK—airport. At this point, I begged off and started a new company of my own, the Metal Container Corporation, a cousin to the White Metal company. Charlie teamed up with Bob Rose to operate as Willis-Rose Corporation.

And lo! Not long after they had taken over at Idyllwild, twenty fuel truck drivers—members of the Coal, Gasoline and Fuel Oil Teamsters Union—went on strike . . . their top pay rate, $1.35 an hour, was not enough. The strike lasted 23 days; Charlie worked with the Port of New York Authority to arrange a pro-temps concession, allowing planes operating out of Idyllwild to land and refuel at LaGuardia without paying the customary landing fee. Then, having lost their leverage, the union finally agreed to accept Charlie's offer of $1.50 an hour. (I might note—this was at a time when some of the upstart freight airlines were paying co-pilots $3.00 an hour, and then, only when flying. The fuel truck drivers were paid simply for being on duty.)[2]

Charlie managed Willis-Rose for a couple of years,

expanding operations to more than a dozen airports; after several changes in name and ownership (at some point, a few years along, Charlie decided he didn't want to run a garage for airplanes), the company is still in business.

It took some time, but we did pay off all of our debts.

And, may I add? This entire experience cost us something more than $60,000 in legal fees (multiply by ten . . .) and left both of us with a rather sour opinion of the "friendly" Federal bureaucracy.

By the way . . . only three years later, 1952, every officer and director of winning suitor U. S. Airlines "resigned." Under new management, and after another three miserable years, the company filed for bankruptcy, and disappeared.

CHAPTER TWO

Charlie and I lived out on Long Island, and saw each other often—in part, to lick our wounds and share our frustration. In truth, "the mess in Washington" was a frequent topic for discussion. While we were basically a-political, it did seem that almost twenty years of Democrat administrations had resulted in parochial arrogance and political gridlock. Perhaps it was time for a change, to bring in fresh ideas. And a fresh approach, an entrepreneurial model, for selecting a presidential candidate.

In our judgment, the Republican Party had put forth a pair of second-stringers for the last three elections—no offense, but the neophyte Wendell Willkie, 1940, was a decent man who simply did not ring the bell and New York Governor Tom Dewey (1944 and 1948) did not attract sufficient support from Independents (although 1948 was a close race, the edge went to the man who knew how to campaign, "Give 'em Hell Harry" Truman). Willkie and Dewey both, well, lacked "luster." (Someone—usually thought to be TR's daughter Alice Roosevelt Longworth, but that is now in dispute—said that the mustachioed Dewey "looked like the little man on the wedding cake." Ouch!)

For 1952, the Party needed a candidate who did not

need an "introduction," who could hit the campaign trail already out in front. Our pick: the universal hero, General of the Army Dwight D. Eisenhower. The man who rose from the rank of colonel in 1941 to five-star general in 1944 and who led the Allied Expeditionary Force to victory in Europe. He was so popular that, when he made a post-war visit to his hometown of Abilene, Kansas, 30,000 cheering people jammed into a city with a population of 15,000. And, rather than fade off into the sunset glow of victory, he remained very much in the public eye: he served as Chief of Staff of the Army, then as the (civilian) president of Columbia University, and in December 1950 he was back on duty as military head of the newly-established North Atlantic Treaty Organization (NATO).

Thus, in June, 1951, just a year before the 1952 Republican Presidential Convention. Charlie and I—with no contact with or support from either Eisenhower or the Republican Party—decided to launch a simple "citizen's effort" to coalesce public opinion and make the general a candidate. We knew that all around the country, there were little whirlpools of interest in Eisenhower; our goal was to link them all together by providing a common theme, resource materials, encouragement, and advice—all, to develop a grassroots demand for Eisenhower to seek the nomination, to express that demand in some way as to impress Eisenhower, and above all, to get him to say "yes".

I must note, in passing, that Charlie thought that General Douglas MacArthur, another well-known victor of the war, should be on our list. MacArthur was in the news, for having figuratively thumbed his nose at President Truman—and for being fired, as a result, as commander of the current effort in Korea. His response, made in a letter to the Congress: "There is no substitute for victory," resonated with some on the far right of the political spectrum and soon encouraged him to seek the presidency. I suppose it was one of the things that encouraged Charlie to suggest—for a time—that we consider supporting a MacArthur candidacy. [3]

I disagreed. MacArthur was also known as an austere, dictatorial, potentate. Not a congenial leader, certainly not someone who could work in a profession—politics—where "ability to compromise" (or, the ability to *appear* to compromise) was a necessary part of the kit.

One step at a time. We would open an office in New York, from which we would set up a network, drawing on friends around the country. We asked a few professional politicians, including Pennsylvania Congressman Hugh Scott and Tom Stephens (secretary of the New York State Republican Committee), for advice. Stephens was encouraging, but skeptical, especially when he saw that we were so naive that we didn't even know how Convention delegates were selected. Well, one step at a time. He did say, "Politically, to the rest of the country, 'New York' is a dirty word." So we rented a loft in Hoboken, New Jersey, hired a secretary—who would be, for the next eight months, our only paid staffer—and set to work to develop a nation-wide network of Eisenhower for President Clubs.

We had two immediate priorities: one, find top-level volunteers who would serve as state-by-state coordinators and who would, in turn, appoint county chairmen who would recruit city chairmen who would be given the task of establishing local clubs; and, two, develop a handbook, a manual, to guide the efforts of all.

Charlie and I had a lot of friends . . . from school, family connections, the war, our business, and fellow members of the "Young Presidents Organization". . . and we had no trouble in developing our leadership team. In truth, one connection often led to others and some of our first-line coordinators would count in anyone's book as grass-roots non-political superstars. Northern California co-chairmen were shipping magnate Lewis A. Lapham (president of the American-Hawaiian Steamship Company) and William Hewitt (a director, and later, president of Deere & Company). Winton Blount (later, U. S. postmaster general) became Alabama chairman. Milton Reynolds, founder of the company that introduced the ballpoint pen to America a week after the war had ended, was chairman of one of our Clubs. Lawyer John Lindsay became a key man in New York. New Jersey State Senator (later, magazine publisher) Malcolm Forbes opened an office in Trenton.

I heard that helicopter genius Stanley Hiller—he built his first working model in 1939, at age 15—had started a movement he called "Young Industry for Eisenhower." I went out to California for a meeting, and brought his group into our network. A most welcome by-product was the addition of Hiller's right-hand man, Langhorne Washburn, to our full-time volunteer staff. Lang, who had been a Navy blimp pilot in the war, offered some unusual ideas that will be reviewed later in this narrative. (A hint: see the photo on the cover.)

The model for our *Eisenhower for President Club Handbook* was the *General Foods Sales Manual*, which, for General Foods field staff, covered everything from how to motivate employees to introducing new products. The basic techniques—pure marketing and public relations —were easily adapted to our mission.

We adopted a loose-leaf format, so that new material could easily be added.[4] The initial edition included, of course, a general introduction and a statement of purpose, an organization chart, and suggestions on recruitment and employment of members. For example, a mailing to solicit members might include such snippets as:

> The 'Fair Deal' is sure it can't lose. It has hundreds of thousands of government jobs and $80 billion to spend...Taxpayer money to deliver votes.

If you are sick and tired of being taxed for government extravagance, bulging bureaucracies and a host of useless nondefense expenditures. . .

If you don't like traveling further down the dreary road to socialism....It's time for a change.

Let's get Eisenhower drafted for President.

We offered a major section on "legal liabilities," alerting to relevant federal and state laws. For example, in some states, Clubs might have to register the names of officers and file all expenditures; however, since Eisenhower was not yet a declared candidate, that requirement might not yet be in effect in some states. Confusing? You bet; we strongly urged Clubs to include lawyers in the membership.

There was a series of "How To" instructions: how to hold a meeting; how to organize a petition drive (and to what purpose); how to arrange a public round-table discussion, how to stage a rally or organize a parade; how to work with local media; and, how to write a press release—with the aid of a few included templates, such as:

An Eisenhower for President Club was launched in *(name of city or town)* today as supporters of the General called upon interested voters to join in a mass demonstration urging Ike to become a candidate for president. . . . By such a demonstration of the people's interest in the candidacy of General Eisenhower, we feel he will make his services available to the country in these critical times.

We sent reprints of newspaper and magazine articles: "Where Ike Stands" from the *Reader's Digest,* an article written by Hugh Scott for the *Christian Science Monitor* ("30 Reasons for the Nomination of General Eisenhower") and a *Business Week* article, "It Takes Strategy and Money To Make Presidents"

We assembled a starter kit of promotional materials: a 6' x 3' "We like Ike" banner, a 5' x 3' picture of Ike (both, for hanging at Club headquarters) and 500 "I like Ike" buttons. We offered the kit for $32; funds received by us were immediately turned around to procure more materials. We included pricing and sources for additional supplies: "Ike" buttons, $5.85 per 1,000; car stickers, $2.80 per 1,000; pamphlets, "The Man Who Can Brings Us Peace," $10.00 per 1,000.

We suggested that the more ambitious Clubs might look to the heavens and hire a skywriter. Rough cost, $125 to write the message "We like Ike" three times in a row. To get more bang for the buck, they could hire a pilot to tow a banner (approximately 34 letters) at a cost of $70 per hour, chock to chock.

And, we included a catalog of other campaign items we had for sale: "I Like Ike" banners, matchbooks, and T-shirts. Those items—like the handbook itself—were sold at cost to our network. We did enjoy some other support—Jack Straus, president of R. H. Macy, donated some office equipment—but Charlie and I were financing day-to-day operations—rent, a secretary, travel, telephone and other utilities to the tune of perhaps $2000 a month.

I must note, we easily adopted and promoted the slogan, "I Like Ike," but many published reports to the contrary (including Charlie's *New York Times* obituary, March 21, 1993), we were not the creators. Eisenhower supporters began wearing "I Like Ike" lapel buttons as early as 1946.[5]

Let me review, some of *that* history. Read on.

CHAPTER THREE

Since the war, Charlie and I had been pretty much absorbed in creating, running, and then trying to salvage our business; we were dimly aware of efforts made by others, going back at least eight years, which focused on a possible Eisenhower candidacy. However—as we later learned and which I include here for context—most of those had been through the direct personal contact with the general by "influential" citizens, and the few efforts that reached out for public support were scattershot, un-coordinated, and made little headway. All of those I mention here were cited in Eisenhower's own 1963 memoir, *Mandate for Change* (which is where, truth to tell, I learned of some of them for the first time, long after Ike had left the presidency).

Perhaps the first attempt to get his attention was a 1943 suggestion by United Press European correspondent Virgil Pinkley, that Ike might well follow in the "presidential" footsteps of successful wartime leaders George Washington, Andrew Jackson, William Henry Harrison, Zachary Taylor, and Ulysses S. Grant. "Virgil," Ike cautioned, "you have been standing out in the sun too long." Ike also reported that in the same year, the American Legion "Tank Corps" Post in

New York City endorsed him for the presidency, and home-state Kansas Republican Senator Arthur Capper planned to place Ike's name in nomination at the 1944 Republican National Convention until Ike said, please don't.

And President Truman, visiting Eisenhower in Berlin, 1945—just at the end of the war in Europe—told Ike that he would help him get anything he might want, "including the presidency in 1948." Startled, Ike treated it as a joke. "Mr. President," he replied, "I don't know who will be your opponent for the presidency, but it won't be I."

Other efforts: in December, 1947, advertising executive John Orr Young (of Young & Rubicam) placed an ad in the Connecticut *Westporter-Herald* calling for a "grass roots" effort to support an Eisenhower candidacy; thirty-five Eisenhower clubs sprang up throughout the state . . . evidence of Ike's popularity, but not much else.

Early in 1948, Leonard V. Finder, publisher of the Manchester (NH) *Union-Leader* asked Ike for permission to enter his name in the forthcoming New Hampshire primary. Ike, by then Chief of Staff of the Army, replied:

> The necessary and wise subordination of the military to civil power will be best sustained . . . when lifelong professional soldiers, in the absence of some obvious and overriding reasons, abstain from seeking high political

office. . . . In any event, my decision to remove myself completely from the political scene is definite and positive. I know you will not object to my making this letter public to inform all interested persons that I could not accept nomination even under the remote circumstances that it were tendered me.

And, make it public, he did. However, soon thereafter, Ike took that job as president of Columbia University. Some people assumed that the change in status might signal a change in his position. It did not, at least in the near term. Among other things, as a five-star officer (a level then shared with nine other officers in the Army, Navy, and Air Force) Ike was on permanent active duty and drawing his full Army pay and allowances no matter what his civilian employment. Nonetheless, radio commentator Walter Winchell asked his listeners to urge Ike to seek the 1948 Republican nomination. In the first week, the Columbia mailroom was swamped by some 20,000 cards and letters.

Popularity, to be sure. Ike was flattered, but was not moved, and moved on.

But he also turned the 20,000-item trove over to Columbia's Bureau of Applied Social Research for analysis, which revealed Ike's support among independent voters: only eleven percent of the writers indicated any party affiliation or preference and eighty percent said they would support him whether he ran as a Republican or Democrat. Very few seemed to care about his views on public or political policy—they, quite simply, "liked" Ike. [6]

It was during this "Columbia" period that Eisenhower actually laid down some of his views on public policy, and they were so cogent that they would be every bit as relevant, today. Let me offer a few examples.[7]

In his inaugural address at Columbia, October 12, 1948, he said.

> The concentration of too much power in centralized government need not be the result of violent revolution or great upheaval. A paternalistic government can gradually destroy, by suffocation in the immediate advantage of subsidy, the will of a people to maintain a high degree of individual responsibility. And the abdication of individual responsibility is inevitably followed by further concentration of power in the state.
>
> Government ownership or control of property is not to be decried principally because of the historic inefficiency of governmental management of productive enterprises; its real threat rests in the fact that, if carried to the logical extreme, the final concentration of ownership in the hands of government gives to it, in all practical effects, absolute power over our lives.

To a Columbia College Forum on Democracy:

In those days [of my youth in Kansas] we didn't hear so much about the word 'security,' personal security through life from the cradle to the grave, some kind of assurance that we were not going to have to go out with a tin cup or sell apples on the streets. But there was constantly around us the right and the opportunity to go out and do better for ourselves. (Feb. 12, 1949)

From an address to the American Bar Association, St. Louis:

Our freedom from degrading pauperism is due to America's deep-seated sense of fair play translated into adequate law; to American industrial initiative and courage; to the genius of the American scientist and engineer, and to the sweat, the organizing ability and the product of American labor in a competitive economy. It is not the result of political legerdemain or crackpot fantasies of reward without effort, harvests without planting.

Some among us seem to accept the shibboleth of an unbridgeable gap between those who hire and those who are employed. We miserably fail to challenge the lie that what is good for management is necessarily bad for labor; that for one side to profit, the other must be depressed. (Sept 5, 1949)

And, at a Carnegie Institute Founder's Day celebration in Pittsburgh, he warned:

If the times demand a sudden and tremendous increase in the budget for defense, reckless extravagance, selfish grabbing, heedless spending of dollars we do not possess will make American citizenship in the future a mortgaged existence rather than a joyous privilege. If solvency and security are not synonymous, they are so closely related that the difference, if any, is scarcely discernable. (Oct 19, 1950)

Need I say? Ike was not only popular, but prescient. As he stepped out on the public stage, Charlie and I had easily sensed the common sense and humanity of the man. Then, in December, 1950, Ike took a leave of absence from Columbia to accept that appointment as the first military head of the new North Atlantic Treaty Organization (NATO), with headquarters near Paris. This was not a casual job-change: NATO needed a firm but flexible leader, someone to bring the various national elements into harmony. And Eisenhower was the overwhelming choice of all.

CHAPTER FOUR

By summer's end, 1951, the Eisenhower for President Clubs were approaching critical mass, and Charlie and I no longer had time for day-to-day on-site management of our regular jobs. We did keep in touch by telephone but only rarely visited our other offices.

Or course, our Clubs and Hiller's "Young Industry for Eisenhower" were not the only organized public efforts, and to our mind, the more the merrier. An "Eisenhower for President" group was formed a few months after ours, headed by Kansas politicians and personal friends of the general, with headquarters in Topeka. A New York City-based "Youth for Eisenhower" sprang forth, headed by Robert W. Sweet. (Some years later, Sweet became deputy mayor of New York City.)

And—of course—private efforts continued. In September, Massachusetts Senator Henry Cabot Lodge visited Ike's Paris headquarters to discuss the presidency. The general tried to turn the subject back on Lodge: "You are well known in politics; why not run yourself?"

Lodge replied, "Because I cannot be elected," and launched into an argument for change that would be every bit as timely today: to end the "steady accumulation of power in Washington, increased 'paternalism' in government's relations with the citizens, constant deficit spending, and a steady erosion in the value of our currency." Lodge urged Ike to allow his name to be placed in the upcoming primaries. However, Ike was still the reluctant suitor . . . although, he left the door open just a bit when he told Lodge, he would "think the matter over." [8]

In November, Lodge—along with Ike's former deputy General Lucius Clay, immediate-past Republican presidential candidate Governor Tom Dewey, Dewey's former campaign manager Herbert Brownell, and Long Island Republican leader Russell Sprague— merged their interests with those of the Topeka group and opened an "Eisenhower for President" office in New York. They saw themselves as more or less the official campaign committee—for a campaign without, as yet, a candidate. They designated Lodge as presumptive campaign manager.

Let me, at this point, set the electoral stage. To many observers at the time—in politics, in the media— Eisenhower supporters were whistling into the political wind. Yes, we were attracting public attention, Ike was popular, but . . . he was not the anointed one, not the clear choice of the corporate Republican Party. That mantle fell on Robert Taft of Ohio—son of President William Howard Taft and himself a senator in his third term. He was known, then and now, as "Mr.

Republican."

Taft had tried for the presidential nomination in 1940, losing to Willkie, and again in 1948, more narrowly losing to the man he considered his political nemesis, Tom Dewey. The two were polar opposites: Dewey (who now supported Eisenhower) was a moderate/liberal, Taft (who opposed Eisenhower) was a hard-over isolationist. He had argued against U. S. entry into World War II; he condemned the Nuremberg war-crimes trials as an extra-legal exercise of the victors over the vanquished; he did not believe that the Soviet Union posed a major threat to world peace, and opposed the implementation of NATO as provocative and unnecessary. On the other hand . . . to his credit, in what seems to be a bit of a contradiction, he supported the establishment of, and the shipment of military aid to, the newly independent state of Israel.

Well, we—collectively—could sing Ike's praises to the heavens or wherever, but the supporters of "Taft" controlled the electoral monologue.

Well . . . one step at a time.

Toward the end of November, Ike traveled to Washington DC for NATO-related discussions with the president and others; upon arrival, he was beset by a throng of reporters who "outdid themselves" trying to draw him into a discussion of politics. Exasperated, he told them:

> . . . as of this moment, I am trying to do a
> job, my staff is trying to do a job, and we think
> it's important, and we think that each of you
> would have a right to resent it if we would try
> to divert ourselves . . . from that job to talk
> partisan politics or state a partisan preference.[9]

The managing editor of the American Federation
of Labor (AFL) monthly magazine asked Ike to "outline his views" on such matters of interest as Social
Security, national health insurance, and Federal aid to
education. Ike stuck to the position that he would discuss no matters that did not "pertain directly" to his
responsibilities at NATO. [10]

There were two reasons—one legal, one personal—
that he now so consistently avoided public discussion
of things political. Army regulation 600-10 prohibited
direct or indirect participation in a political campaign
"or any other public activity looking to the influencing
of an election or the solicitation of votes for themselves or others." And Eisenhower simply didn't see
himself an active political campaigner. At some point,
he did tell a friend that if he was nominated, he would
work to win the election. This was the signal for which
his friends had been waiting.

Interesting to note: unknown to us at the time,
Truman repeated his 1945 "offer" of the presidency. He knew that Eisenhower's position on foreign
relations was much closer to that of the Democrats
than that of the generally-isolationist Republican

Party, and his election would be a sure thing. Truman appealed to Ike's sense of duty, to do whatever he "thought best for the country." Ike responded, he was a Republican, had always been a Republican, and could not abide Democrat public policy. [11]

In a December poll of Republican members of the House of Representatives, Eisenhower ran behind Senator Taft, with fifty-four votes to Taft's seventy-one. [12] Behind . . . but not bad for a non-candidate being measured against the professional politician generally acknowledged to be the Party's favorite, supported (as noted in the January 27, 1952 *New York Times*) by "a machine that has been continually in existence for more than a decade. It abounds in experience, technicians and that essential lubricant, money."

The first-in-the-nation presidential primary would be in New Hampshire, March 11, and the period allotted for putting a name on the ballot was January 11-30. It might seem like a simple move—except New Hampshire required affirmation of the political affiliation of the nominee, and no one knew whether Ike even had an affiliation. New Hampshire Governor Sherman Adams checked with the county clerk in Ike's home town of Abilene, who responded that

Mr. Eisenhower has never voted in this county as far as I know . . . his father was a republican and always voted the republican ticket up until his death, however, that has nothing to do

with the son as many differ from their fathers
of which I am sorry to see. . . .The multitude
believes in going into debt and see how much
they can spend, it has become a habit and will
sink the nation into bankruptcy. [13]

I assume *he* was a Republican . . .

In a letter dated December 17, Adams posed
the question to Senator Lodge, "to which party does
General Eisenhower belong?" Lodge responded that,
during conversations while Ike was at Columbia, "he
specifically said that his voting record was that of a
Republican. He also pointed out that his political
convictions coincided with enlightened Republican
doctrine and that the family tradition was Republican
. . . . I therefore authorize you to enter the name of
Dwight Eisenhower in the [New Hampshire] primary
election." [14]

Done.

CHAPTER FIVE

When we heard that Lodge had been picked as campaign manager, Charlie and I asked for a meeting. We wanted to let him know what we had been doing . . . we soon would have almost 800 "Ike" clubs in 38 states . . . we wanted to continue, but, well, we were about out of money and needed help.

Lodge was very cordial. In truth, he had experience in the "grass roots" division of politics. When he first ran for the senate, 1936—at age 34—he was the only Republican in the nation to win a senate seat from a Democrat. And he got the nomination by courting delegates, one-on-one, in their living rooms or kitchens for more than a year. Lodge told us to keep up the good work—but suggested that we shift our operation to New York, the better to coordinate with a number of other players. He also urged us to set-up a more formal organization, to take on an executive with administrative experience, and to work with a professional fundraiser.

Well, OK, we were team players. We established a corporation, "Citizens for Eisenhower." For the executive, Lodge had just the man: Arthur Vandenberg, Jr., who had spent more than a dozen years as executive assistant and campaign manager for his late father, a Republican Senator from Michigan. Junior Vandenberg soon became chairman of Citizens for Eisenhower, and we added Mary Pillsbury Lord as co-chair. Financier John Hay "Jock" Whitney became chief fundraiser, Sidney Weinberg, the head of Goldman Sachs (and, a Democrat), became treasurer, and Robert P. Mullen—PR director for the post-war Marshall Plan and a former editor for the *Denver Post*, the *Christian Science Monitor* and *LIFE* magazine—soon came aboard as press secretary. Mullen's former boss at the Marshall Plan, Paul Hoffman (recently appointed head of the Ford Foundation) signed on as an advisor.

We quickly saw that Vandenberg was neither energetic nor organized enough for the job, and by the middle of March he was eased out and over to a face-saving role as an assistant to Lodge. In his place, we added Seattle banker, Chairman of the Council on Economic Development (and unsuccessful Republican candidate for the Senate, 1950), W. Walter Williams.

By the end of January, with most of our new team in place, we had moved our headquarters to the Marguery Hotel, East Forty-seventh Street at Park Avenue. The then-vacant building, slated for demolition, was owned by an Eisenhower fan, and space was therefore rented to Citizens at a very favorable rate. In a corollary effort, Youth for Eisenhower erected a tent in the parking lot (over which they hoisted a sign, "DRAFT IKE BOARD No. 1" and from which they launched a phone-bank operation). We now had room to grow

. . . and soon had some 700 volunteers working at the Marguery, many of whom had simply walked in and said "What can I do?"

One was FDR's youngest son, John Roosevelt, who wanted to help, and volunteered in the office, but at this point (in his life, or in the campaign) he felt it was not wise for him to come forth and be revealed as a Republican. Later, after Ike was the official candidate, John publicly went to work on his behalf.

FDR's son John Roosevelt, proud supporter of the Republican candidate at a press conference announcing a three-week speaking tour on behalf of Eisenhower.   [UPI]

Another visitor was Kay Summersby, the former British Army soldier (and by then an American citizen) who was Ike's driver and secretary during the war. She wanted to volunteer. I said "Miss Summersby, the most helpful activity you could undertake would be to stay out of sight." Any indication that she was involved with the campaign would surely restart the rumors that had circulated toward the end of the war, that she and the general were having an affair. To the best of my knowledge the rumors had never been substantiated but such is the nature of gossip that substantiation is irrelevant. (Sure enough, as Ike's candidacy became real, the rumors indeed re-surfaced, perhaps being steered by some Taft supporters. They went nowhere.)

One walk-in was rather unusual: Gabriel Hauge had been, among other jobs, professor of economics at Princeton and assistant editor of *Business Week* magazine. He earlier had been involved to some degree with the Dewey-Lodge group seeking to engineer an Eisenhower candidacy, and wanted to help. He became our research director. His first task was to find all of the scurrilous comments attributed to or attached to Eisenhower. Ike was either anti-Semitic or Jewish (he was neither). He was accused of serious errors of command during the war (when the "errors" were the result of policy agreements among the Allies). He either was playing a game by pretending to be disinterested in the nomination, or he was too arrogant by half, demanding nomination without his active participation. (I don't think that Ike had, just yet, really studied the proposition).

Another project: to research Taft's voting record

and his stand on various issues. This information—direct quotes only, no interpretation—was indexed by topic, and given to Eisenhower Club leaders in the field.

Some folks wanted to know where Eisenhower stood, for example, on civil rights or economics, and Gabe set to work on a brochure, drawing on those speeches that Ike had made while at Columbia. We soon learned, however, that most people did not seem to care where he stood on anything: they simply liked the man and just *knew* that he would be a great President. (Ike, himself, was flattered but a bit frustrated; after a planning session with a group of politicians, he told Governor Adams, "All they talked about was how they could win on my popularity. Nobody said I had a brain in my head.") [15]

And I must acknowledge another walk-in—although he had not dropped by to volunteer. Gilbert A. Robinson, a recent graduate of Roanoke College, had been working on a 30-part syndicated newspaper series, "Why I Like Ike," and Walter Williams was one of the contributors. Gil needed final approval on the copy, and he asked Bob Mullen to pass it in to Williams. Bob did so, and asked Gil would he like to come aboard and work with him at "Citizens for Eisenhower," perhaps help out with some publicity? Gil—then a young man with a narrow focus—said, "Gee, I still have some columns to finish." Bob asked, how long might that take? Gil replied, "Couple of weeks."

So Bob closed the deal. "All right, tell you what. Start with me today as my assistant . . . while you finish the columns." And so he did—learning the craft of political public relations from the ground up. (Not to get too far ahead of my story, but now-retired *Ambassador* Robinson is the publisher of this small memoir of the campaign.)

I had noted, earlier in my narrative, that we welcomed any and all "For Eisenhower" clubs and organizations to the cause . . . "The more, the merrier." Well, I spoke a bit too soon. There was a great deal of confusion in the news media, which mistakenly put us all under the same organizational umbrella. Yes, "Citizens" was aligned with "Youth for Eisenhower" and "Young Industry for Eisenhower" and we were all pulling on the same oar. . . but in truth, we were not at all happy when we were lumped in with the at-the-time official but dysfunctional "Eisenhower for President" group. Lodge and his team were certainly savvy politicians and leaders, but were scrambling to get organized . . . eight months after we had opened our modest doors in Hoboken. They had been waiting for some encouragement from Eisenhower and were playing catch-up ball; we had been focused on encouraging the general and knew what we were doing, from the start.

A dysfunctional "Eisenhower for President?" Examples? Sure, for the record . . . because no book or report I have yet to find actually sorts it all out and my goal in creating this narrative is to offer accurate and demonstrably successful advice, support, and guidance to future electoral efforts.

At the very moment "Citizens" was moving into the wide-open spaces of the Marguery, the *New York Times* (I must note, an Eisenhower supporter) described "an air of unreality" at the headquarters of "Eisenhower for President" — "a hastily evacuated apartment in the plush uptown Shoreham Hotel . . . . Paperwork spread out over the kitchen cabinets and electric stove; women volunteers busily addressing envelopes by hand on shaky card tables."

"Eisenhower for President" was charged—gently, I suppose, as a school-teacher might nudge a student— with "haphazard publicity operations." There was no real PR plan, casual mailings included randomly selected reprints of favorable news articles, editorials, and cartoons sent to a list of 15,000 Republican workers throughout the country. There were no speech writers (or, even, designated speech givers), and the group was unable "to produce a press release except under the most urgent necessity." They were getting support, the newspaper reported, from a scattershot group of "organizations" that included a great number of "spontaneous and uncoordinated groups of well-wishers lacking the sort of discipline and control that spells political effectiveness." [16]

I must say, the general description was not all that far off the mark. But Charlie and I were not exactly thrilled to be known as members of a "spontaneous and uncoordinated" group "lacking the sort of discipline that spells political effectiveness." We were first out of the gate; we had a plan, we knew that we knew how to do what we wanted to do . . . and were doing it. I will admit . . . we may have been a bit naive, PR-wise, more focused on our goals—recruiting Eisenhower enthusiasts—than generating flattering press notices. However, we were so far ahead of the "professionals" that we were not going to be goaded by a newspaper.

Things began to move rather quickly. Ike's growing popularity was having an impact . . . especially on the Taft forces. Just as we were moving our office, the Republican National Committee held its annual meeting, out in San Francisco. Dave Ingalls—Taft's cousin and chief strategist—acknowledged that opponents would say that Bob Taft "lacks color and glamour." His response: "To this I say, he has the color of ability, the color of experience, the color of courage . . ." He went on: "Hero worship is no substitute for faith based on known performance. Neither is glamour or sex appeal." Fair enough, but then he made, in my judgment, one of the dumbest political analogies, ever. "If we as a party," he said, "at this late date, propose to risk our political future on such slender attributes, then I say the party is dead and we are met here today merely to select a good-looking mortician to preside over the final rites."

When it came his turn to speak, Senator Lodge began with a simple declaration. "I shall speak for my candidate," he said, "and I shall never attack any other candidate." Then he reminded his audience of some facts of political life: with only about 31 percent of voter registrations, there were simply not enough Republicans to elect a president without additional support. They must have a candidate, he said, with the broadest popular appeal to Independents and to Democrats as well as Republicans. A candidate, that is, whose "hold on American opinion" goes well beyond "a warm personality and a magnetic bearing," but is grounded in his demonstrated knowledge and skill in dealing with matters of war and peace." [17]

That got my vote . . . and set the direction of the campaign.

On January 21—at almost the moment that political warriors Ingalls and Lodge were tilting at the RNC lists—President Truman submitted a budget with a $14 billion deficit, and about three weeks later, February 8, eighteen prominent Republicans—including former-President Herbert Hoover and Senator Taft— urged that American troops should be brought home from Europe. Was the country headed for bankruptcy or isolation . . . or both? According to one biographer, Ike was furious, something had to be done and he was moving closer to a decision.[18] The tipping point was set-up on that same day, February 8, with "Citizens" smack in the middle of the most significant event of the pre-convention season . . . the event that, more than any other, brought Ike aboard as a candidate.

CHAPTER SIX

New York PR professional John Regan (better known as "Tex") McCrary and his actress-model-tennis star spouse Eugenia Lincoln (better known as "Jinx") Falkenberg—the couple, known far and wide as "Tex and Jinx," for the daily radio show they hosted—decided to throw a party, a big party, for Eisenhower supporters. They would develop a program to be held at Madison Square Garden; Tex had already staged several such events at the Garden, and for one of them, saluting the Air Force Association, Eisenhower—then at Columbia—had been the official guest of honor. [19]

This was to be a party with a purpose, not simply to entertain the visitors but to demonstrate the range and depth of public support for an Eisenhower candidacy . . . directly to Ike. Planning started at the end of December, 1951. Jock Whitney met with Jacqueline Cochran (world-renowned aviatrix and key figure in bringing women pilots into non-combat service with the Army Air Corps) and invited her to be co-chair of the rally. She was at first skeptical. "Where are we going to get the money?" Whitney told her not to worry it would be taken care of: her job was to involve her connections and create interest. She remained skeptical. She checked with the management at Madison Square Garden and learned that successful political rallies at the Garden were rare, not even for local candidates, let alone for someone who had not even declared. Well, she signed on. Perhaps it was the challenge.

"Citizens" was invited to join Jackie and help fill the venue . . . maximum seating capacity 18,500 . . . and soon enough we had enough program information to start building interest among possible attendees. Appearing and/or performing would be Clark Gable, Mary Martin, Ethel Merman, Irving Berlin . . . you get the idea.

However . . . our task was not as simple as you might think: the program couldn't start until at least 11:00 pm, because the Garden was already booked for a regular Friday night prize fight earlier in the evening. Thus, we were inviting folks to come from far and wide by car, bus, air, and special train (one, chartered by a Texas group set up by Jackie, brought horses) to attend what would essentially be an all-night event; "professional" politicians scoffed at the whole idea; we would never fill the place, they said, it would be a major embarrassment and would certainly slow any "Eisenhower" momentum.

Well, call it an embarrassment of riches. Our guests not only filled the Garden—chanting, "We Like Ike!"—but many of them could not find a seat because a) we had done such a good job in attracting attendees and, b) because many of the spectators for the prize fight knew what was to follow and decided to just remain for the party. "We like Ike, too!" they chanted.

Now, to this day, I do not know if this was happenstance or on purpose: why was our event scheduled for that particular Friday night? Some years later, several members of our team each claimed "credit"— they said, they wanted to ensure a full audience and just *knew* what would likely happen, the folks already in the arena simply would stay in their seats. I don't know, and it's a good story, but, well, it's a little late to make inquiry to set the record straight

In any event . . . it was a big mess. No one really knows how many people were crowded into the arena or how many were left on the concourse or even outside in the chilly but not frigid evening— no published report agrees with any other. I've seen numbers as high as 50,000 (absurdly fanciful) and as low as 20,000. Our best guess at the time: 20,000 in the arena, 10,000 outside (they could follow the program on loudspeakers). A bonus audience: the show was broadcast on both radio and television, with popular broadcaster Bill Stern providing "color commentary."

But the program . . . was great fun, if at times a bit clumsy. A group from New Hampshire (home of that "first-in-the-Nation" Republican presidential primary) kicked off the show with a parade, led by "Miss New Hampshire" wearing a bathing suit. A delegation carried a sign, "TAFT FOR EISENHOWER." (They were from Taft, Texas). A chorus sang "Battle Hymn of the Republic" accompanied by an American Legion drum and bugle corps. Ethel Merman sang "There's No Business Like Show Business."

Jinx Falkenberg batted Ike-branded tennis balls from the "stage" (i.e., the boxing ring) while Humphrey Bogart and Lauren Bacall greeted the crowd. Mary Martin—who was in London and joined the party by short wave radio—sang "I'm in Love with a Wonderful Guy" accompanied on the piano by composer Richard Rodgers who was in the Garden.

Clark Gable introduced Irving Berlin, who sang a new version of his song "They Like Ike," which had been written for the 1950 Broadway musical "Call Me Madam." A snippet:

> Tried and true,
> Courageous, strong and human
> Why even Harry Truman
> Says "I like Ike."

Whereupon, an actor portraying President Truman stepped forward, in character and costume, to great laughter and applause.

As I mentioned, our purpose was to demonstrate—to our candidate—the range and depth of support for his candidacy. Therefore, the entire program had been put on film, and Jackie Cochrane—somewhat, I think, to her surprise, as this had not been part of the bargain— was tasked to take it to Ike's headquarters in Paris. She booked an overnight flight on TWA (an upper bunk in a sleeper section; forget the common report that she flew solo in her own airplane). Ike's quarters included a small movie screening room, and Ike, his wife Mamie, and some staff members watched the film, somewhat in awe.

"It was a moving experience," he was later to write, "to witness the obvious unanimity of such a huge crowd—to realize that everyone present was enthusiastically supporting me for the highest office in the land . . . . the incident impressed me more than had all the arguments presented by the individuals who had been plaguing me with political questions . . ." [20]

When the film ended, Eisenhower asked Cochrane if she might like a drink? She thought that might be quite nice. Then, when she had been handed her glass, she raised it with a toast, "To the President." Whereupon Ike was so overwhelmed that he literally burst into tears.

Jackie told him, "I'm as sure as I'm sitting here and looking at you that Taft will get the nomination if you don't declare yourself. There's not going to be a draft of you sitting here in Paris."

He thought about that for a moment, and then said, "This is what I want you to do. I want you to go and see General [Lucius D.] Clay and tell him to come over and see me." He said that Jackie could tell Bill Robinson (publisher of the New York *Herald Tribune*) and Jock Whitney that he was going to run—the timing, to be determined, he had work to do at NATO—but this was all to be treated as "top secret." The King of England (George VI) had just died, and Ike suggested that Clay might meet him in London after the state funeral (scheduled for February 15) which would provide cover for the mission.

Jackie had no trouble meeting with Robinson and Whitney but had the devil of a time in getting an appointment with Clay. He was then chairman of the Continental Can Company, and the palace guard was virtually impregnable. Jackie once joked, that she could call the President of the United States—any President of the United States—and get put through, perhaps after some scheduling delay, but she couldn't get past General Clay's secretary. Finally, after several days trying, with the State Funeral fast approaching, she lost her temper and told the secretary that if she could not see General Clay *he* would regret it for the rest of his life and she—Jackie—would see that the secretary was fired. Well, that worked; at their meeting, Clay seemed rather bemused, especially when Jackie asked him to come with her down to Grand Central Station where there would be no possibility of eavesdropping. There, she told Clay that Eisenhower was "going to run for the presidency." His reaction? Jackie said later that, if Clay had false teeth, he would've dropped them on the sidewalk. [21]

I think that Jackie may have been exaggerating, a tad, because Clay had long been involved in "presidential" discussions. But Clay did make the trip to London.

CHAPTER SEVEN

Charlie and I may not have understood the "delegate selection process" when we started on our crusade, but we were quick learners. Most Nominating Convention delegates were selected through state conventions or a caucus process, where concerned citizens met in living rooms or other suitable spaces to argue about and vote for their favorites. Sixteen states held presidential primaries and eight of those permitted write-in entries. A caucus was important, but a primary served as a training ground for the get-out-the-vote-machinery of, and a test of the public interest in, each candidate, and thus attracted attention well beyond the borders of the individual states. Our volunteers roamed the streets of the nation soliciting signatures on petitions urging an Eisenhower candidacy . . . petitions that could be useful in having his name placed on some primary ballots (the rules varied, from state to state).

Of course, a primary election offered a great opportunity to practice classic grass-roots organizing. Start with a phone bank: "We're having a meeting for the Eisenhower campaign. Would you be interested in joining us for lunch?" Then, out of that group, they would recruit precinct workers and then the precinct workers would recruit block captains and the block captains would canvass their neighborhoods. And sell Ike buttons and neckties (which they would buy from us) to pay for pamphlets and other support literature.

Our team had started "organizing" the primary vote, but Taft was actively campaigning and drawing good crowds; Ike was in France, not likely to return home for some time, and his surrogates—Senator Lodge, for example—would not by themselves draw much of anything. So Lang Washburn and another new volunteer, Art Gray, formed a "special events" division as part of "Citizens," with their first events kicking off the Eisenhower campaign in the New Hampshire primary: they set up a series of rallies, with professional entertainment. Tex McCrary's role did not end at Madison Square Garden; he was active in lining up the entertainment. For example, band-leader and well-known choral director, Fred Waring, might stage a musical program, Jinx Falkenberg might bat out a few more tennis balls, Eisenhower's wartime mess sergeant, Marty Snyder, would pass out recipes for Ike's favorite onion soup, and a comedian or two would warm up the crowd that had gathered for the show. On occasion, Governor Sherman Adams was not shy to join in, singing some tunes of the day while accompanying himself on the piano. And then came the "Ike for President" pitch. [22]

An editorial in a pro-Taft newspaper complained that "vaudeville" had no place in politics. "Comedy and Choruses have nothing to do with picking a president of the United States. . . it's an insult to the voters." [23]

It was just at this point that we expanded our information program—at the suggestion of Cabot Lodge—with the assistance of some professionals from the Young & Rubicam advertising agency. They assigned a manager full-time to the effort, Frederick A. Zaghi. His first target: voters in New Hampshire, to persuade them to vote for Eisenhower. Fred then visited other primary states, meeting with the head of Citizens in each, to assess possibilities and determine requirements (as in, brochures, newspaper advertising, radio spots). He came back from a visit to West Virginia and said, we could forget that state, they were so hard over for Taft that we would just be wasting money.

We had "state chairmen" in 38 states, and everyone had a story to tell. Here's one: Floyd Oles, our man for the state of Washington, had been personally recruited by Hugh Scott (at the suggestion of Governor Arthur B. Langlie). Oles was a long-time Taft supporter—he had been, in fact, the state campaign manager for Taft in 1940 but had been out-of-the-country on Army duty during the 1944 and 1948 elections. Well, other than the governor, almost all professional Republicans in the state were Taft fans, but Oles knew that Ike would be the better candidate. So he accepted the challenge, and began planting stories with the newspapers. As you will appreciate, he got a lot of grief from local politicians . . . but also, from Ike's brother Edgar, who lived in Tacoma. Edgar—who Floyd had never met—

called and chewed him out. "God damn it, you've got to stop this! I don't want my brother running for President." Oles gave back as good as he got: "I don't give a good God damn what you think about it. I'm starting a campaign and if you don't like it you know what you can do." And hung up on Edgar. And through a series of county conventions and then the state convention, he wrangled twenty of the twenty-four state delegates, for Eisenhower. [24]

Floyd and Edgar soon enough became friends, but in one of those weird footnotes to history that make life so interesting, Ike himself later recalled that a classmate had written in his 1909 high school yearbook, that Ike would grow up to be a professor at Yale and his brother Edgar . . . would be President of the United States! [25]

The New Hampshire primary was held, March 11, on a cold, wet day—with a record turnout. Result: Eisenhower 46,661, Taft 35,838. We were off to a good start.[26]

McCrary had another, albeit silly, role to play during the primary campaign. Senator Taft had written a book on foreign policy and was invited to appear on the NBC television show "Author Meets Critic." The critic: Tex McCrary. His first question: "Senator Taft, how can you write a book on foreign-policy when the only time you've been out of the country was on a vacation trip to Bermuda?" It was to be the only question, as Taft stormed out of the studio. Taft demanded that Tex be fired; David Sarnoff, head of RCA (which owned NBC) invited Tex to drop by for a chat. Because NBC depended on federal licensing, Sarnoff could not take the risk of offending a senior senator and potential president, and gave Tex a choice: resign or be fired. Tex resigned, whereupon Sarnoff said, "That's fine. And here's my personal check for the campaign." [27]

As you will appreciate, there was a lot of pre-convention skirmishing between Taft forces, who largely controlled the delegate-selection process, and the Eisenhower supporters who often managed a work-around. Such as, with the March 18 Minnesota Republican Primary. Our team petitioned to have Ike's name on the ballot; the state Supreme Court rejected the application on a technicality, whereupon we launched a write-in campaign. Ike scored 108,692 write-in votes; former governor and favorite son Harold Stassen, whose name was on the ballot, got 129,076. (Taft was an also-ran with 24,093 write-ins). This was pretty good evidence of the value of our get-out-the-vote effort—especially, for a man who was not yet an "announced" candidate.

At least one primary—Nebraska, April 1—threw out any write-in where the name was misspelled. We tried for "voter education." We failed. "Taft" (with 79,357 write-in votes) won over "Esinehower" and "Eisenhouter" or whatever (66,078 valid votes). We knew that some spelling-challenged Ike supporters voted for Stassen—his name was on the printed ballot

and the voter could just check a box with an "x." In
one sense, we won: Ike and Stassen together, call it the
"anti-Taft" vote, polled 55 percent of the total and
Taft had just over 36 percent. But, of course, he won
the delegates. [28]

In May, we combined the special events division with
Stanley Hiller's "Young Industry For Eisenhower"
(YIFE, headquartered in Palo Alto), to operate as part
of the "Citizens" organization. Charlie and I became
members of the management group, which also
included, I might note, Charles H. Percy (president of
Bell & Howell and later, Senator from Illinois), Robert
P. McCulloch (the chain-saw king), Raymond Hickok
(founder of the Young Presidents Organization),
and John Fox (co-inventor of frozen orange juice
concentrate). Langhorne Washburn was designated
field secretary—which meant to us, he was in charge
of operations. We treated YIFE as a mobile task force,
free to step in at a moment's notice to solve problems
or execute initiatives.

General MacArthur was an announced but not effective
candidate, usually as a write-in who usually drew less
than 1 percent of the vote; eventually, he read the
tea-leaves and stopped promoting his own candidacy.
On June 1, he endorsed Taft for the June 3 South
Dakota primary—the last in the cycle. MacArthur was
influenced, I later learned, by an offer from former
President Herbert Hoover and the Taft team to make

him the keynote speaker at the Convention, and to put him on the Taft ticket as the vice-presidential candidate. He did become the keynoter; there was, of course, no Taft ticket. [29]

"Citizens" sent public relations expert Abbott Washburn to manage that primary in South Dakota. Taft was a very active campaigner, Eisenhower was not allowed on the ballot and write-ins were not accepted, but former Governor George Mickelson was a candidate, more or less acting as a place-holder for Ike. The campaign slogan became "A vote for Mickelson is a vote for Eisenhower." Washburn organized teams of volunteers to go from house to house, and discovered that the younger folk among them coveted the Ike campaign badges, with which they would decorate their jackets, the more buttons the better. He was delighted to let them have as many as they wanted—it was cheap advertising.

Well, Washburn reported that the Taft forces spent time on some underhanded tricks, one of which, to the best of my knowledge, was a series of radio advertisements directed at the large ethnic German population in the south of the state. With great inaccuracy, they accused Eisenhower of "turning German soldiers over to the Russians." [30] We lost. But by only 600 votes.

The Primary box score: Taft, 2,794.736 votes; Eisenhower, 2,050,708 votes. Taft won 6 primaries, Eisenhower 5, and Governor Earl Warren of California and (as noted) Harold Stassen of Minnesota, one each.[41] And just at this point, Ike came home to join the fray.

And he—literally—hit the ground, running. On June 4, he gave a televised homecoming speech in Abilene; his remarks were, well, awkward, rather all over the place, his hopes, dreams, plans for the future and advice for the present, and so forth. (A member of Congress from Tennessee—a Taft supporter—gave a short critique: "It looks like he's pretty much for home, mother, and heaven.") [32]

Advertising agency BBD&O, which had long worked for the RNC, stepped in with some basic suggestions. You want to give the impression, they said, that you are "talking to people, as one frank, unassuming American to his fellow Americans." In other words, ditch the prepared script, just talk, and if you want to be sure to hit all of the points you intended to make, put them on a note card for quick reference. [33]

At a press conference the next day, his first as a true candidate, Ike was much more relaxed, this was a forum with which he had long been comfortable. There was a bit of controversy, at the start. The print reporters did not want the conference to be covered by the TV folks—they already had their shot with the speech the day before—and complained to Ike's press secretary, Bob Mullen. The TV folks put in their own bid. Ike settled that nonsense. As long as the cameras do not interfere, they stay. [34]

While in Abilene, Ike met with Convention

delegates from six states, hoping to enlist their support; then, off to New York City for meetings with twenty more delegations. Staff-prepared briefing books gave Eisenhower a head-start on the meetings—offering bits of personal information on the delegates (how many kids they had, their golf score and handicap), things Ike could easily focus on and easily turn into a pleasant moment.

During a session with a group from Pennsylvania he was asked whether he was prepared to wage an "enthusiastic" campaign, he snapped back that this was a "funny kind of question to put to a man who has spent forty years of his life, fighting." It was during a meeting with the New Hampshire delegation that he first met Governor Adams, who had been playing such a key role. [35]

Then, on to Denver, his wife's home town and his choice for the location of a campaign headquarters. He was greeted by a crowd of 100,000 cheering fans, and began non-stop meetings with more delegations and with special-interest groups largely seeking reassurance that he would support their causes. We—and in this, I include the other campaign organizations—created many subgroups, where a logical affinity would bring people together. There were Lawyers for Eisenhower, Bankers for Eisenhower, Doctors for Eisenhower, Volunteers for Eisenhower, Mothers for Eisenhower, Democrats for Eisenhower, German-Americans—and any ethnic group you can imagine—for Eisenhower. We also had working contacts with some twenty-five national groups (as dissimilar as the American Legion and the National Council of Negro Women) which were not identified as Eisenhower supporters, but were interested in the campaign and were happy to offer suggestions. When Ike met with representatives of affinity groups, he usually had a tailored message; for example, when speaking to doctors, he emphasized his disapproval of socialized medicine.

June 26 was designated "Eisenhower Day" in Denver—Ike gave a speech to 11,000 fans in a stadium and an untold number in the radio and TV audience, many of whom were Eisenhower Club members gathered around the nation for fund-raising dinners.

Next, it was ten days on the road during which he gave nine speeches and then, on to Chicago, site of the Republican nominating convention. He arrived July 5—to begin another constant round of delegate-stroking.

CHAPTER EIGHT

Going into the Convention, Taft was leading— according to the Associated Press, with 530 delegates to Eisenhower's 427—but did not yet have quite enough delegates (604 required) to win on the first ballot. The question: how to get Eisenhower to come out on top? Ike's team had a two-part answer: hoopla and strategy.

"Hoopla" was pretty much what "Citizens" had been doing since February, creating interest and generating enthusiasm. Now, the first week in July, we wanted to pack the Convention hall with as many non-delegate but vocal Eisenhower supporters as possible—but there was a problem. The Convention was, in theory, open to the public but access was tightly controlled by the Taft forces. Art Gray and I (who had been sharing a hotel room in Chicago for a full month before the Convention) were looking for "opportunities," and Art discovered that the leader of the company that provided entry control and security for the venue, Andy Frain, was an Eisenhower man.

Eureka! Andy set aside one entrance, to be under his control, through which a couple of hundred of our demonstrators could freely pass, without a Taft-issued ticket. At appropriate times—as, when Ike's name was

mentioned—they would break out signs and banners and parade around in loud and grand style, joined, of course, by the pledged Ike delegates already in the hall. Call it, momentum, and make a note: it works . . .

As the Convention got underway, Eisenhower Clubs around the country urged members to telegraph their state delegations, calling for support of Eisenhower. Soon enough, bags of telegrams began arriving on the convention floor, much to the delight of the Eisenhower supporters and the distress of the Taft clique.

"Hoopla" was not, of course, limited to the Convention Hall. We also held street-corner rallies and filled the city with cheering throngs. We wanted to make a good first impression on all delegates arriving for the convention, and had teams of people assigned to cover the airport and each of seven railway stations in downtown Chicago. Their mission: to greet the delegates, shake hands, offer carnations, beverages and snacks (which were to be purchased, if possible, from vendors on the spot; we did not want "Eisenhower" to be blamed for taking revenue away from concessionaires); thus, to send the delegates on the way to their hotels with a good feeling. The "Operation Greeting" teams were equipped, of course, with Eisenhower banners, all wore "I like Ike" buttons, and name badges. All members were told to maintain a friendly demeanor, smile a lot, and make no comment critical of Senator Taft. Where feasible, a brass band was assigned to stir up excitement at each station.

How many people were involved in this activity? Hundreds, with one team assigned to meet each group of delegates and each team ranging in size from three to eight members (attractive women and courteous children, especially welcome). I don't know the total, but I do have one "arrival metric." When Ike got off *his* train at Chicago, he was met by 10,000 cheering fans. All arranged, courtesy of "Citizens for Eisenhower."

Just before the convention got underway, Ike agreed to meet with some folks who just wanted to shake his hand. As it turned out there were some 6,000 of them and the reception went on for hours. Ike did not flinch. "They came to see me," he said.

Our Young Industry for Eisenhower (YIFE) division was given the lead on special hoopla, and Lang Washburn—as noted above, a former-Navy blimp pilot—had a brilliant idea: he created 40-foot long floating aerial billboards, using war-surplus helium-filled barrage balloons with "IKE" or "WIN WITH IKE" painted on the sides in letters seven-feet high. Not cheap: the balloons cost less than $200 each, but the helium was $600 per inflation. It was money well spent. By day or night (illuminated by huge anti-aircraft searchlights) the balloons could be seen from miles around. Lang dubbed the nighttime version, his "ENS," for "Ethereal Nocturnal Spectacle."

[Photo: Bettie Zacher]

At Chicago, one IKE balloon was floated outside the window of the office of Colonel Robert R. McCormick, owner and publisher of the *Tribune* newspaper and a highly-vocal supporter of Taft. Someone—most likely,

[Photo: Bettie Zacher]

a *Tribune* staffer—took exception to this implied insult, and shot down the balloon. Lang proceeded to heal the wound while an angry squad of local police were ordering him to take the balloon away, it was blocking traffic, whatever. He took his time and, once patched, the balloon was refloated. Again, outside Colonel McCormick's office. I don't recall any official inquiry into what most certainly must have been a firearms violation of some sort. The government of Chicago was, more or less, not on the Ike team.

When Lang was ready to shift the venue—he wanted to move the balloon and his support-truck a

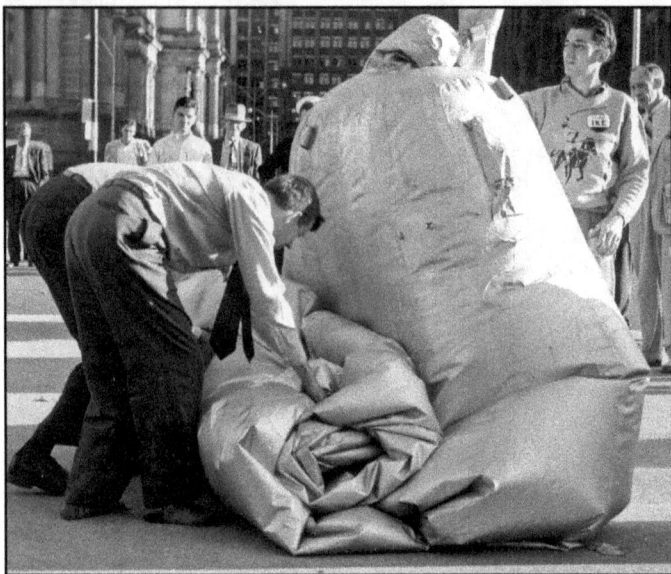

Langhorne Washburn repairing the wounds inflicted on an IKE balloon by an outraged anti-Ike partisan in Chicago.   [Photo: Bettie Zacher]

mile or so straight south, to float outside some of the hotels that housed delegates—he was told that trucks were not allowed on Michigan Avenue and the city would not give him a permit. So he flagged down a pair of motorcycle cops, told them he needed an escort to the Hilton Hotel, and just started driving . . . and they fell into line. Lang also brought in a sign-carrying helicopter—something of a rare bird at the time—to attract more attention. It was all great sport, balloon and helicopter, the talk of the town, and that was what we wanted, to keep a focus on Eisenhower.

We of course had obtained a list of all the delegates, and the names of the hotels in which they were staying (along with their room numbers). Zaghi and his Young & Rubicam team prepared persuasive "Vote for Ike" hand-outs to be slipped under the room doors—and then discovered that the hotels frowned on such activity, at least, during normal working hours. There was a simple work-around: a bevy of attractive young ladies, bearing hand-outs, would arrive at 2 in the morning and charm the doormen into letting them pass. [36]

There had been flawed delegate-selections in Texas, Georgia, and Louisiana, where the Taft forces had hi-jacked the process and now were being challenged by Eisenhower supporters. The solution: first, shame the miscreants with a loud call for "Fair Play" (our demonstrators paraded around the hall bearing signs, "Thou" "Shalt" "Not" "Steal"). In a coup, of sorts, Fred Zaghi arranged for television coverage of the first debate, centered on Texas, which greatly discomfited the old guard; they would have preferred a discussion behind closed doors in a traditional smoke-filled room.

After "hoopla" came "strategy," managed by Ike's campaign team, with a bit of parliamentary sleight-of-hand. The credentialing committee was induced to decline certification of the contested delegates by blocking any contested delegate from voting on the status of contested delegates from any other state. This helped level the playing field, so to speak. (I don't mean to make this seem easy or simple; it was not. But it worked.)

Ike was nominated on the first ballot. And, in the

[Photo: Republican National Committee]

best example I can think of, as to why he deserved not only the nomination but to win the election, he made his first order of business to seek out Bob Taft, even before the delegates had left the hall, and ask for his advice . . . and support.

The next order of business was to select a vice presidential candidate. Eisenhower had a little list of "possibles," but didn't have to go past the first name: Senator Richard M. Nixon of California was the clear favorite. The political calculus was basic. Eisenhower was almost 62, Nixon was 39. Eisenhower was now identified with the East Coast, Nixon with the West coast. Eisenhower had no legislative experience, Nixon had been elected to the Congress in 1946 and 1948, and to the Senate in 1950. And Nixon was a tenacious anti-communist, which certainly appealed to many voters.[37]

Another choice to be made: who should be the campaign manager? The logical candidate was Lodge, who had been filling that role leading up to the Convention, but Lodge was now to be thoroughly involved in running his own campaign for re-election to the Senate. Art Summerfield, as head of the RNC, became the titular campaign manager and Sherman Adams—taking a leave of absence from his job as New Hampshire's governor—was appointed chief of staff. At the urging, I am sure, of Tom Dewey, the governor's press secretary, James C. Hagerty, became press secretary for the Eisenhower campaign (and served as presidential press secretary through both of Ike's administrations). He replaced Bob Mullen, who took over public relations at Citizens, a role in which his exceptional range of media contacts came into play. If Bob had an idea for an article or editorial for, say, the *New York Times*, he just got on the phone and talked with the editor. Not just *an* editor, but *the* editor.

Hagerty asked Y&R to shift their efforts from Citizens to working for the "official" Eisenhower campaign. OK. Young & Rubicam developed the outline for a print advertising campaign, citing what they called "clear-cut" issues to be addressed: inefficiency, corruption, high prices, and high taxes. Stevenson should not be the target; apparently, even President Truman had told Stevenson "The only thing you have to run on is the record of the Democratic party." Wonderful! That record, Y&R urged, "should be played with all the effective repetition of a cigarette commercial, until no voter in the land can fail to understand the point." The theme:

> Let's clean house! ... You can't clean house with a worn out broom! ... Only a Republican... Only Eisenhower can clean house in Washington.[38]

I might note, that Sigurd Larmon, Chairman of Young & Rubicam, joined Charlie and me as a fellow vice-chairman of Citizens and we spent many hours working on advertising strategy. So, even though the Campaign was now driving that boat, we were playing in the same pond. And—as you will see a few pages along—Citizens soon became involved with another ad agency in the 20th Century breakthrough effort in political advertising: the television spot commercial.

CHAPTER NINE

After the convention Mary Lord, Walter Williams, Charlie Willis and I were invited to the Denver campaign headquarters for a meeting with Art Summerfield, Chairman of the Republican National Committee. He had a plan of his own: "Citizens" would thenceforth operate under the auspices and control of the RNC. Well, that was a non-starter; we knew that the Independents and Democrats we had been attracting to the Ike camp would simply fade away. We told Summerfield, "Thanks but we'll go our own way. We will coordinate our activities with you, but there's no way you can tell us what to do." And we went back to New York, and got to work on the campaign.

One nice interlude: Citizen's officials from around the nation converged in New York to meet Eisenhower. It was a joyous occasion, perhaps 300 enthusiastic amateurs cheering the non-professional candidate. Ike exulted, "Boy, this is where I belong!" [39]

We began charting a course, searching out pockets of voters where some extra attention might pay off. We made a precinct by precinct study of voting patterns with a focus on the big cities that were usually carried by Democrats, especially those where the margin of victory had been small. As Lodge had noted at that January RNC annual meeting, Republicans alone could not elect a President: we needed Independents and disaffected Dems.

Now that Ike's candidacy was official, we had to re-organize, to meet new legal requirements. We closed our operation—and opened another, "Citizens for Eisenhower-Nixon" under the same management. And, of course, our focus shifted from "encouragement and nomination" to "get out the vote." The current Eisenhower Clubs were re-branded Eisenhower-Nixon (and, because some of our supporters thought that "Club" sounded too casual, we allowed them to use "Committee" instead). And YIFE became, well, YIFEN.

We issued a new and updated "handbook," which offered current Eisenhower positions on a wide range of topics including Foreign Policy, the Korean War, Communism, Corruption in Government, Inflation, Waste, Civil Rights, Socialized Medicine, and a Citizen's Duty to Vote. These were direct quotes from Eisenhower, not edited or enhanced by some staffer, and were provided to assist the Eisenhower-Nixon Clubs/Committees with their speaker's programs and publicity efforts. And, we added a number of relevant get-out-the-vote functions to the organization, including conducting house-to-house canvas, working the telephones, running election day car pools, and stationing poll watchers and challengers. Elections can be won—or lost—by failing to cover all of the bases.

We urged supporters to "show their colors" by posting an "I Like Ike" message on their cars and homes, to discuss the election with their friends and neighbors (with an emphasis on candidate Eisenhower), to drop by the local Citizens for Eisenhower-Nixon office to offer help, and to make sure that they themselves were registered to vote. It was amazing to learn, along the way, how many politically-vocal citizens were not, in fact, eligible to vote . . . because they had never registered!

The Eisenhower campaign headquarters—still in Denver—began receiving, on average, between 2000 and 3000 letters a day. Ike insisted that unless they came "from cranks or nuts" all should be answered; it was a matter of simple courtesy that he had always followed. "I see no reason," he said, "in altering that policy now." Well ... Abbott Washburn took up that challenge, organizing hundreds of volunteers to prepare and mail the answers. The letters covered issues from Mamie's hair-style (bangs) to offshore oil—some of which could be handled by a simple form letter, some requiring a more personal approach, but all were individually typed and addressed.

When members of the press—a naturally suspicious breed—heard reports of the deluge of correspondence, they thought someone was just hyping Ike's popularity. So they were invited to open some mailbags and take a look. Then, it was not long before the RNC became apoplectic over the bills for postage

—which of course they were obligated to pay because Eisenhower was, after all, the candidate. They sent a note to the campaign staff; they had "never had a candidate who spent so much on direct mail." Ike told the staff, "Tell them they haven't had one for 20 years that got elected, either!" [40]

I can tell you with certainty that this "letter writing campaign" paid off; everywhere Ike went, people would come up proudly waving the letter "he" had sent them.

The official campaign—Ike vs the selected Democrat contender, Illinois Governor Adlai Stevenson—was to begin just after Labor Day (September 1), but it would seem foolish to sit around, waiting, and Ike had some visits he wanted to make, including the Veterans of Foreign Wars convention in Los Angeles (August 5), a large Native American gathering in Gallup, New Mexico (August 10), the Western Governor's Association in Boise Idaho (August 20) with a visit to Kansas City the next day, and an appearance at the American Legion Convention in New York, August 26. With that, Ike shifted his campaign headquarters from Denver to NYC.

Boise was a good test of "Citizens" new "5 for Ike" telephone pyramid scheme: 50 volunteers would divide up the phone book, and each would call five people who would be asked, in turn, to call five more listed in the same section of the phone book, each of whom would call another five . . . until almost every-

one in town had received a phone call, urging atten-
dance at an upcoming Ike rally in front of the Idaho
State capitol. I suspect that many people got more than
one phone call, but no matter, 19,000—in a town of
34,000— turned out for the rally. Of course, we knew
that some of the enthusiasm shown by crowds, in one
place or another, was to salute the war hero who had
never before visited their town, but enthusiasm is con-
tagious and the war hero easily morphed into the presidential candidate. [41]

Ike's remarks to the VFW, the Native Americans,
and the American Legion were basically non-political,
but what he said in Boise has resonance yet today:
"For every evil of government, they [the Democrats]
propose more government. To reach every social goal,
they know only one means: a newer, bigger, more
highly centralized bureau in Washington." [42]

At one point—and I don't remember the date or
place—Ike made a speech . . . and no one was there to
hear it. Well, of course I exaggerate, but do so to make
a point: the audience was rather thin, even though the
speech had been promoted on local radio and in the
newspaper. Lang and Art worked their magic . . . and
thus was born an actual and not figurative Bandwagon:
a 25-ton branded semi-trailer, which carried a loud-
speaker-equipped Jeep (which would lead a parade),
one or more barrage balloons, tanks of helium, anti-
aircraft searchlights for illumination, 500,000 "I Like
Ike" buttons, and two dozen Ike dresses (designed by

[Photo: Bettie Zacher]

Art Gray's wife Adele—one half would be worn at an event while the other half were being cleaned to be used at the next town). The Ike girls would ride on the fenders and in the Jeep, passing out the buttons. The Bandwagon travelled with a caravan of other vehicles carrying the support crew, which included four volunteer drivers for the big truck.

The Bandwagon would pull into a town—one or two days ahead of an Ike event, to meet up with the advance man who was already on the ground. The "advance" would coordinate with local Republican officials and any local Eisenhower Clubs, set up a volunteer phone-bank operation, sign up eight "Ike" girls, obtain a few tons of confetti for dropping from high buildings, plant stories with the local media, and hand radio disc-jockeys and news directors recordings of the official campaign song, "We Love the Sunshine of Your Smile" (a slightly-revised version of a then-current pop song, featuring the Pied Pipers, with Marc Carter and Orchestra).

> We love the sunshine of your smile.
> We see our future in your eyes.
> You led our men to victory.
> You are the one we idolize.

Then, the Bandwagon would put on a show. There would be a parade—usually at noon, and in most places it was a welcome diversion, the carnival come to town. However, there were several cities—Chicago notable among them—where the reigning politicians sent the cops out to harass the participants, who simply ignored the cops and continued on their way (and the cops, many of whom we surmised were sympathetic to Eisenhower, let them do so).

First came the Jeep, bearing an announcer with microphone: "Ike is coming to town! Tonight at the Municipal Auditorium! Come one, come all!" Then a marching band leading the Bandwagon, with the Ike girls tossing out buttons, then another band or two or three (all, thanks to our musical coordinator, 28-year-old Elizabeth Firestone—yes, of the tire family). Wherever possible, at least one band was a professional (union) group, and the members would be paid. Several Mummer's bands marched in Philadelphia, and of course the New Orleans parade was enlivened by a couple of traditional jazz bands.

Also—wherever possible—an elephant would participate, carrying or wearing an "I Like Ike" sign (we preferred baby elephants, but adults were welcome . . . either one, clearly intelligent and instantly lovable and representing, of course, the symbol of the Republican Party. I don't recall many Democrats trotting out donkeys . . . a stubborn and noisy animal . . . the unfortunate symbol of their Party).

With high fanfare and great media coverage, an "IKE" balloon would be inflated and sent aloft at the site where Ike would speak. Launching a 40 foot long barrage balloon (or, as Lang Washburn called it, "throwing up a bag") was quite an operation. First step: inflate the bag to about the three-quarters mark, then mount the top and bottom tailfins. Step two: have four men grab hold of the steadying lines and finish the inflation. Step three: when the balloon has reached the desired altitude, anchor the primary mooring line to, say, an automobile. A caution: about a dozen feet of the bottom of the mooring line should be steel cable to prevent sabotage by hostile forces.

The searchlights would be lit, and the Ethereal Nocturnal Spectacle would charm viewers throughout the night. I was told that, at an event in Cleveland, the balloon could be seen from a distance of thirteen miles. If someone didn't know that Ike was coming to town, they must have been in a coma . . . well, again, I exaggerate. Once, I asked a cab driver if he knew

[Photo: Bettie Zacher]

what was going on, and he said, "I dunno, something, I guess."

I wrote, "Bandwagon," but as we went along, we added two more units so that one of three "Bandwagons" were always on one road or another, leap-frogging to ensure that our candidate's visits were well-covered. As you will appreciate, it took much longer to advance a visit than for the candidate to make the visit.

It also consumed a lot of helium. One day, we had a phone call from a dentist with a complaint: he needed some helium, and couldn't find any because it seems we had cornered the commercial market. Well, we certainly helped him out . . . and I hope, although it was not a condition, won him as a voter.

LIFE magazine asserted that "No previous campaign has ever produced anything quite like" the team of Washburn and Gray, and applauded their "brass, bravado, entreaty and sheer enthusiasm....Their bandwagon was fueled with high octane exuberance" as they "helped mobilize some of the biggest crowds in the history of political roadshows." [43]

Grand praise, well deserved. But . . . I must note that Mullen brought in another Time-Life veteran, Jack Beardwood, to handle press relations. Beardwood had been head of the *LIFE* bureau in Los Angeles and then was an editorial director for Time, Inc. Do you wonder that "Citizens" got such tremendous coverage?

Lang and Art went to work with more confidence than most local political leaders. Let one example stand for all. The official kick-off of the campaign was September 4, where Ike was scheduled for a rally and speech at Philadelphia's Convention Hall. The event was sponsored by the Young Republicans led by the National Chairman, Pennsylvania State Chairman, and Philadelphia Chairman of that organization. The three men were prominently mentioned in all promotional materials (along with a plug for "youth" . . . "Never before in history has a Presidential candidate opened his campaign with an address to YOUNG AMERICA").[44]

Our simple rule: give people a title, let them exercise it, and they will repay you with great energy.

These were men with solid political connections and experience: one was a (successful) candidate for the Congress in the forthcoming election; another was a long-time member of the Pennsylvania State Senate; the third was a three-time delegate to Republican Presidential Conventions.

We got the "energy" . . . however . . . they didn't quite know what to make of "Citizens for Eisenhower." The capacity of Convention Hall was around 18,000. Lang and Art asked for outside loudspeakers to accommodate an expected overflow crowd. The event sponsors scoffed, they doubted that the hall would even be filled. Lang and Art insisted; the pols gave in. Guess what? The Hall was jammed, and 20,000 people stood outside—a larger crowd than had ever been drawn by Roosevelt, Truman, or Dewey.

The Philadelphia Plan ran 39 pages, filled with information about the Bandwagon parade, the candidate's motorcade route (including minute-by-minute timing and suggested alternates to accommodate the unexpected), details of local issues for discussion, and a program of special events along the way—for example, there would be a visit to the Liberty Bell, where the candidate was to "place his right hand on the bell and pose for pictures." Lang and Art had scouted the location; at that time, the Liberty Bell was in a rather confined space and the only decent pose for a photo was, "right hand on the bell" so the candidate would be facing the cameras.

Supplies on-hand for the rally? 3000 noisemakers, 5000 flags, 25,000 programs. The Plan also offered brief bios of local politicians and dignitaries the candidate would be meeting (along with perhaps one or two old Army buddies); the team would have weeded out most supplicants pleading for "just a few moments" with Ike—typically, publicity hounds, professional gate-crashers, and inventors of secret weapons.[45]

CHAPTER TEN

Overall, the bandwagons traveled 35,000 miles through 26 states; Ike himself, by train and air, covered 51,000 miles and visited 232 cities and towns in 45 states (skipping only Maine, Vermont, and Mississippi).[46]

This was the first time that "air" had been used in a presidential campaign. For some travel, the "party" might number fewer than twenty—the candidate and Mamie, a physician, speechwriters, a communications specialist, someone to keep track of everything, and some security. In those days, the Secret Service was not involved; typically, a few retired police officers would be in the party, and on the ground, local police details would be assigned to the candidate.

But for most travel, after you added the press (including equipment—cameras, lights, baggage), there might be two or sometimes three plane loads . . . and getting three planes to take off at the same time could be a problem. Say, you charter three DC-6 four-engine propeller-driven airplanes; if one engine wouldn't start, none of the planes would take off, they had to be held back so they all would travel together. Happened at least once . . . to the distress of the planners . . . who were often involved in a coordinated mating dance of sorts—back and forth, often air for one leg of a journey, campaign train for another.

A travel coordinator—Walter Swan, on loan from United Airlines—was always with the candidate, whether in the air or on the ground, to manage schedules and accommodate changes. Changing schedules for a charter flight was relatively easy for the airline—they just needed to file a flight plan with the FAA and notify the target airport. It was rather complicated for the railroads which allocated passage—passenger, freight, maintenance, and special trains—on firm fixed schedules well in advance. As a further complication, the Campaign train was operated by New York Central, but often ran on the tracks of other operators. Somehow, Walt always made it work. [47]

The advance team—the schedulers, the folks who determined how long it might take to go from A to B, from airport or train station to an event venue—knew that their best estimates were always subject to such variables as, a) weather b) overly large friendly crowds c) an opposition demonstration blocking the route d) an unrelated traffic accident or e) a flat tire, and even if A to B went as planned and all was ready for the candidate's close-up, the public address system might fail.

In my experience, the team hovering around and controlling the candidate were lawyers and politicians and similar obsessive-compulsive types. They expected perfection. The schedule would be met! The team really running the show were the PR folks like Bob Mullen and the businessmen—Walter Williams, Jock

Whitney, Charlie and myself—who knew that nothing ever really went as planned. And, of course, in a similar vein, there was a large component of military-professionals—including the candidate—who always hoped for perfection but knew that hope was not a strategy.

Now, how does all of this play out, in the real world? Say, you are the on-scene coordinator in charge at an event . . . the candidate is making his closing remarks but is far from the end and you know the timetable is running down, he will have to move out NOW! Do you send in a staffer to tug at his elbow . . . TIME TO GO. Not a pretty image, not for the adoring crowd, certainly not for the observing newsmen. Therefore . . . the schedulers always fudged the schedule, fifteen minutes here, twenty there, and never shared the "fudge" with the campaign team. Brilliant.

The campaign train was configured for eighteen cars—including sleepers for the permanent staff, media, and train crew/hospitality support; there was a coach for short-term passengers, a private car for Ike and Mamie, a club car, three diners, a laundry car, a fully-equipped rolling office, and, of course, the observation car at the end of the train with the outside-platform from which the candidate would greet crowds assembled. It was not practical to break the train down, say, to nine cars for one leg, build it up again for another . . so it was eighteen, all the way all the time.

At each stop, an on-board telephone switchboard

would be hooked up to a network and a communications team would be busy making and taking calls . . . until the train next left the station. A teletype was installed on the train and in at least one hotel room whenever the traveling team was not spending the night on the train. The teletype (call it, an electric typewriter joined by radio signal or phone line to another electric typewriter at Campaign headquarters) was the link to the outside world, bringing news reports, copies of Stevenson press releases and speeches, and guidance from the RNC. Of most value: speech drafts bounced back-and-forth between headquarters-based speechwriters and the travelling staff.

The team of speechwriters was necessarily large, perhaps eight or nine at any given moment, because fresh speeches were needed daily, at times almost hourly. While a major evening speech would certainly provide a fresh opportunity to make a statement, even the whistle stop speeches had to vary somewhat one from the other. The audience on the ground—one town from the other—wouldn't notice, but the traveling press corps would. Just imagine the headlines: "Ike has no fresh ideas." On the other hand . . . there were only so many topics to be covered, and the more important were necessarily repeated, time after time. Call it, a juggling act.

There were some issues with the speechwriters—they were all "professionals" of one sort or another (journalist, columnist, educator, whatever) but the style of most was too pedantic or formal—they would have been a good fit, stylistically, with the patrician Stevenson, but not the country-boy Ike. He was not comfortable with stilted rhetorical style; the advice given by BBD&O after the Abilene speech fit quite nicely with Ike's preferred modus. In fact, for many presentations, he would review the final version of the speech until he was comfortable, and then use 4 x 8 cue cards to remind him of the high points—and to provide him with the names of his hosts for the event and of various dignitaries in the audience; this may have been the most important part of the exercise. In any event, Ike was his own editor, engaging in frequent "dialogue" (albeit, often by teletype) with the speechwriter of the hour. Over time, more and more of the speech-writing and tweaking fell to Gabe Hauge, who—more than any of the other men involved—understood Eisenhower.

Either Charlie or I were always on the train with Ike. We weren't baby sitters, we were coordinators, always in communication with the advance team, looking for glitches or opportunities (of which, on both counts, there were often a few). A typical "whistlestop"— where the candidate would wave to the crowds from the train's rear platform and deliver a few stirring re-marks—might last seven minutes, then it was on the way to the next stop.

The major events were usually in the evening, a speech wrapped in a rally. The scene post-speech in any town was often chaotic. Well-wishers wanted to get close to the candidate (who desperately wanted to get back to the train) and traffic was often a mess, so much so that some of the staffers who had been in the audience for the speech were unable to get back to the train ahead of the candidate, who usually had a police escort. When Ike stepped aboard, the train got underway. The folks left behind had to scramble to catch up, one way or another.

[Photo: Bettie Zacher]

The "whistle stops" themselves did not always go as smoothly as planned—or as hoped. On one run through Michigan in early October, the train was a few minutes late but the engineer, determined to remain on the published schedule, pulled out of the station before Ike could say much more than "Ladies and Gentlemen…" The engineer was soon replaced with a less-obsessive driver with a bit more common sense.

Each time the train moved from one stop to the next, it carried a travelling squad of local politicians from that next town, who came aboard for the ride and the opportunity to brief the candidate. They also would enjoy the opportunity to be seen getting off the train in their hometown, thus illustrating their strong personal connection with Ike.

One traveling staffer, Homer Greunther, bore a slight resemblance to Eisenhower—he was about the same size and build and slightly bald, and when the train was passing through small communities where hundreds of people might be lining the tracks to wave at the train as it passed, Homer would stand on the back platform and wave back. If the train was moving at 30 miles an hour or greater the con was undetectable; at slower speeds, Homer could not pass for Ike. Interesting to note, members of the traveling press corps were fully aware of this mild deception, but to my knowledge, no one reported the story until after the election. [48]

When the train arrived at a scheduled stop, we met up with any Bandwagon that may have advanced the visit . . . and, schedule permitting, while the candidate was off to make a speech, we afforded some good food, rest and relaxation time for that crew. If the train was going to remain at a stop for a while, the volunteers might catch a nap—or more—before we had to move on.

Understand, the Bandwagon crew were *all* volunteers, not a paid professional among them . . . including the drivers, who were just some volunteers willing to drive a truck (I do believe that some if not all had relevant experience, perhaps in the Army). Well I remember . . . one "truck driver" who was, in the real world, the top executive at some business. He wanted to catch up on some sleep, we put him in a roomette on the train . . . and then Ike wanted to meet all of the volunteers who had come aboard for that stopover. Well, I knocked on the roomette door and after a few moments it was opened by a very sleepy guy. I said, to him, "I'd like to introduce General Eisenhower" and the volunteer replied, "Excuse me, sir, I didn't quite get your name."

A few pages back, I offered a comment on "security" —it was not until 1968, in reaction to the killing of Robert Kennedy, that the Secret Service began protecting presidential and vice-presidential candidates (they had been covering the Presidents since 1902). In the 1952 campaign, Eisenhower was, well, wide open to any mischief; let one example suffice. A manager at a hotel where Ike was staying wanted to pay his respects but wasn't sure how to get past the doorkeepers, who were screening out thrill seekers and other nonessential visitors. Well, dinner was being served in Eisenhower's suite and the manager simply told one of the waiters to loan him his waiter-coat, and pushed in a food cart. You get the idea . . .

Some of Ike's "advisors" urged him to avoid the South, it would be a waste of time and money. He went anyway. The Democrats of the South were incensed by this political invasion of Dixie, and branded Ike a "decoy" for the South's "traditional enemies."

One governor (Gordon Persons, Alabama) advised his fellow Southern Democrats to stop referring to Eisenhower with such friendly or honorific labels as "Ike" or "general," but to start calling him what he was—a "Republican." From a Southern-Democrat point of view, I suppose that was pretty good advice.[49]

In any event, Ike reminded his advisors that the President is president of all the people and even if he didn't win the Southern vote, he needed to understand their issues and problems and show the citizens that he cared.

He went places where the Republican Party was virtually invisible, and drew crowds—in large part, because of the Bandwagon effect. In addition, he went places (in and out of the South) where the local Republicans had been solidly behind Taft and resented his presence—places where I believe some local Republicans would rather lose the election than put Eisenhower into the White House. They had promises to keep to their supporters, some of which they knew an Eisenhower-led administration would never condone. No matter, the Bandwagons put on their show and our candidate spoke his piece.

Let me describe a typical two-day swing, this, in the middle of October. On October 14, our candidate traveled from New Orleans to Houston, by train, arriving 7:30 am for a motorcade, rally, and speech, then off by air to Waco at noon for another speech, then by air to Lubbock at 2:45 for a speech, then by air to San Antonio for a major evening event (which included, in passing, a birthday party for Ike . . . in the state of his birth).

The campaign train was by then waiting in San Antonio; Ike and Mamie spent what was left of the night, to awake for a flight to Ft. Worth the next morning, then to be driven to Dallas and later shuttled by air to Shreveport, Memphis, and Knoxville . . . where, after the evening speech they boarded a plane for New York City. Results? Not to get too far ahead of our story, but in the general election, Ike won two of the three states visited on that swing, Texas and Tennessee, even though his advisors tagged them as "southern." In fact, since the Civil War, Texas had only voted once for a Republican, 1928.

For a moment, imagine, if you will, the range and depth of advance planning that went into each of those (and of course, all other) campaign visits. Here, it was nine cities in two days: local politicians, newspapers, radio, and television reporters to be notified days ahead and given access during the visit; arrangements for ground transportation, crowd control, parade and rally permits; scouting and signing event venues; signing up volunteer participants (phone bank operators and the Ike girls); finding temporary lodging for the advance team, Bandwagon staff and, on occasion, for the candidate and his retinue; preparation of briefing materials for the candidate with special focus on Members of Congress (or fresh new candidates) standing for election. Duties of the advance-teams were shared, one way or another and as necessary from one place to another, between the campaign organization (which had, I believe, six advance men) and our own advance teams working with the three Bandwagons.

CHAPTER ELEVEN

Soon after their own Convention the Democrats began to use the slogan, "You never had it so good!" and Jock Whitney—our chief fundraiser—wondered, how could we best counter that bit of fiction? A friend in the advertising business had a bold suggestion: create short television spots and flood the airwaves. Thus it was that Citizens for Eisenhower-Nixon became pioneers in what would become a sea change in political campaigning.

TV was still rather new on the public scene—but by 1952, there were about 100 active stations and 18 million TV sets, and a modified version of any TV spot could be broadcast on radio, thus reaching pretty much everyone in the nation. Television was being employed, of course, in the news-coverage of the campaign; the Madison Square Garden salute had been televised, as had both of the nominating conventions. But that was passive coverage, showing what was being said and done in front of the cameras.

The candidates did, of course, have some control over the message . . . but no candidates of the day had any real experience in dealing with the medium. As advertising agency BBD&O had suggested, after Ike's first speech in Abilene: give the impression, that you are "talking to people, as one frank, unassuming American to his fellow Americans." In other words, ditch the prepared script, just talk, and if you want to be sure to hit all of the points you intended to make, put them on a note card for quick reference. That was good advice—then, and almost anytime. But not when working within the unforgiving time constraints of television.

Case in point: Stevenson, while a superb public speaker, was not well attuned to time-sensitive issues and would on occasion be cut off in mid-sentence. This was not a problem with Ike . . . rather the opposite, his personal staff usually timed his TV speeches out to the second. Usually. I do recall one farm-belt speech on some agricultural topic where, at the last minute, a staffer insisted it was two minutes too long, and the speech-writer and Ike had to go through the script with a red pencil and cut it back just before show-time. Well, you know what happened. The speech ran out two minutes before the time slot ended.

Jock Whitney's friend Rosser Reeves, of the Ted Bates advertising agency, invited a group from "Citizens" to a meeting in a back room at New York's "21 Club." Walter Williams, Walter Thayer, Jock Whitney, Sidney Weinberg, Bob Mullen, Charlie, me, and about four other associates of "Citizens," were treated to a most persuasive pitch. Radio spot ads had been used in the 1936 presidential race by Republican candidate Alf Landon (he lost) and in the 1948 election of

Chester Bowles as governor of Connecticut (he was an advertising professional, co-founder of the Benton & Bowles ad agency). The idea of TV spot ads was kicked around in 1948, when Dewey considered but rejected the idea. Thus, ours would be the first-ever major political campaign to use spot ads on television.

Reeves noted that big advertisers paid huge sums of money to sponsor television programs perhaps, $75,000 for a one-hour broadcast, with the shows coming one right after another, each having built a big audience. So . . . what comes between any two shows? The humble spot—20 seconds, 30 seconds, or one minute—for a relatively small sum it provides access to the audience built at huge costs by other people. The tactic worked for commodities, why not for political campaigns?

In fact, Reeves had just completed a bit of market research in which he showed a film of MacArthur's convention keynote address to a random audience of 500 people, followed by a one minute commercial spot. On testing, 91 percent of the audience was able to recall the main points of the spot, while only 8 percent could make any sense out of MacArthur's 45 minute speech. Point made. [50]

Reeves had what we saw as rather high estimates of the cost for an effective campaign, such as, $1.5 million for the air time, and high expectations also for the result: his research, he said, told him that a change in voting behavior "of a mere 2 percent in 62 designated counties in 12 crucial states could spell the difference between victory and defeat in a close election."

Well, maybe. But who knows? This was a project for our PR expert, Bob Mullen, and thus, with our support, was born the political spot commercial. Mullen set a goal, to put Eisenhower in as many American homes as possible . . . limited only by how much money was contributed to pay the costs.

I must note that Eisenhower was not sold on the idea of being the star of his own series of little TV shows; at first, he agreed, and then he waffled. Reeves asked him, "Do you think it is all right for a candidate to make a 30 minute speech on television or radio?" The general replied yes. "Fifteen minutes?" Yes. "Five minutes?"

Eisenhower said "I am quite sure a five-minute speech would be in order."

Reeves said, "If we cut that speech to a one minute, is there anything wrong with that?"

Whereupon Ike grinned and said "Okay, let's go ahead."

This colloquy, by the way, was not a spontaneous reaction to Eisenhower's reluctance, but was a well-rehearsed argument Reeves made frequently—and persuasively—when explaining what it was he did for a living, boiling reality down to bits of fifteen- or twenty-seconds. A friend challenged Reeves, "you can't say anything in a fifteen-second speech." Reeves asked, "Do you remember that old radio speech of Franklin Roosevelt—his first acceptance speech?" His friend said yes. "And the phrase about the only thing we have to fear is fear itself?" Again his friend assented. And Reeves said, "That's a fifteen-second spot." Another example: Reeves cited the speech that Winston Churchill gave at Fulton, Missouri, and asked, did his friend remember what he said? His friend remembered, "An iron curtain had descended on Europe." And Reeves, triumphant, announced "That was a fifteen-second spot from Churchill." [51] Reeves is remembered, even today, as the inventor of the concept, the "Unique Selling Proposition" (as in the classic Anacin commercial, "Pain, Pain, Pain—Relief, Relief, Relief.") You get the idea . . .

Topics to be covered? Pollster George Gallup suggested that voters were most interested in the high cost of living, corruption in Washington, and the war in Korea. So the challenge was passed along and the Ted Bates Agency—with assistance from Bob Mullen and several other agencies—came up with a collection of draft scripts for about fifty 20-second spots. Eisenhower's handlers, perhaps disdainful or distrustful of the process, gave Reeves one day of the general's time to film all of the spots. As his advisor—read, "censor" —Ike brought along his brother Milton, who reviewed each script. From time to time, Milton would object to some phrase that had been taken word for word from a speech that Eisenhower had given. "Ike," he said, "would never say this." Reeves would protest, that Ike had already said it, and Milton would close the issue: "He's not going to say it again." [52]

The scripts used a question and answer format. The series was called "Eisenhower Answers America," with Eisenhower looking straight into the camera and answering questions posed by what certainly were typical Americans. [53]

"General, just how bad is waste in Washington?" Answer: "How bad? Recently just one government bureau actually lost $400 million and not even the FBI can find it. It's really time for change."

In another spot a woman complained of high prices, and Eisenhower offered reassurance:

"Yes, my Mamie gets after me about the high cost of living. It's another reason why I say, 'It's time for a change. Time to get back to an honest dollar and an honest dollars worth!'"

Question: "The Democrats have made mistakes but aren't their intentions good?" Answer: "Well, if the driver of your school bus runs into a truck, hits a lamp post, drives into a ditch, you don't say his intentions are good—you get a new bus driver."

You never had it so good? In one spot, Eisenhower noted, "Can that be true when America's billions in debt, prices have doubled, taxes break our back, and we are still fighting in Korea? It's tragic and it's time for a change."

Another, same theme: Question: "Food prices, clothing prices, income taxes won't they ever go down?" Answer: "Not with an $85 billion budget eating away on your grocery bill, your clothing, your food, your income. Yet the Democrats say, 'you never had it so good.'"

And . . . my favorite: "I'm a veteran, general. What's wrong down in Washington? Graft, scandal, headlines, how can you fix it?" Answer: "Here's how. By your votes, we'll get rid of the people who are too small for their jobs, too big for their britches, too long in power."

Amazing what you can pack into 20 seconds.

In production, the order of question and answer was reversed: Ike recorded the responses in a studio in New York—all of them in the allotted one-day session—and then a few days later, the "typical Americans" asked the questions. The text of each spot—questions and answers—was put on large cue cards, to be held up in front of, and read by, each "performer." Ike started out wearing glasses; it was the wrong look—"image" is everything—the glasses were ditched and the cue cards were re-done with LARGER letters.

The typical Americans were recruited from groups taking the guided tour of Radio City, people who came as they were, from wherever and wearing whatever and speaking in their own regional tongue. When all of the material had been sorted out, we—"Citizens"—ended up with twenty-eight 20-second spots and three 1-minute spots (which were merely padded-out versions of three of the shorter spots).

We paid the $60,000 production cost, and Rosser Reeves set up a committee of a couple of dozen well-connected folks to help us solicit funds to pay for broadcast.

Reeves postulated that Dewey lost the 1948 election "by only 35,000 votes." A pretty bold claim, which he supported by noting that those 35,000 votes were cast in 61 critical counties in 12 crucial states, presumably by Independents who made up their minds at the last minute to vote for Truman. Well . . . maybe. But it made a good sales pitch to raise money to pay for broadcast of our spots. In his promotional materials, seeking an "investment in victory," he called it:

> "OPERATION ON-THE-SPOT," an all-out, grass-roots drive, AT VITAL LOCAL LEVELS, to SWING THE "UNDECIDEDS" TO EISENHOWER, in those 61 counties, in those 12 states, between now and November 4th. . . . You can elect Eisenhower by contributing now to "Operation On-the-Spot." The need is great! The time is short! Do it today! [54]

We got the money.

We had "print versions" of the copy points, different from but similar in theme to, the TV spots. They were passed on to all of our Clubs/Committees under the heading, "How to Combat the Democratic Theme, 'You Never Had It So Good."

Who never had it so good? Some examples (from our hand-out):

> The working man who uses his car in his work and must pay 14 cents tax on a 12-cent gallon of gasoline?

> The youth starting out in life who must work one week out of every three . . . just to pay his taxes?

The patriot whose $100 maturity-value war bonds are worth only $48 today in actual purchasing power?

The small businessman who can't get a Defense order because he doesn't have the "right connections" with the Democratic machine?

And, who has had it, "so good"?

The politically-connected Chicago gangster who settled his $890,000 income tax bill for 10 cents on the dollar.

The 174 Internal Revenue employees who were recently "separated" — 53 for taking bribes and 24 for embezzlement.

Etc.

You get the idea.

CHAPTER TWELVE

As noted above, each of the 800 or so Ike Clubs had a program to raise funds—to cover printing, advertising, hosting candidates, paying for phone lines, whatever. They threw parties, held auctions, and we sold them trinkets and printed materials that they could sell to friends and neighbors.

Of course, a significant part of our own campaign was devoted to fund raising—a task that called for experts on law, accounting, organization . . . and human nature. We brought in attorney Walter Thayer as executive director of the Finance Committee (joining Chairman Jock Whitney and about 150 committee members). Fidelity Bank President Howard Peterson became fund-raiser-in-chief, and our goal was to have an experienced head of fundraising in each state.

However, petty jealousies sometimes got in the way, as in California where we not only had to appoint a Northern California and a Southern California committee chairman, but also a "Hollywood" committee chairman, a position for which three movie moguls fought each other to a draw...so we had three Hollywood co-chairmen, none of whom of course would be actively involved in actual fund-raising. They just wanted to have their names on the letters. [55]

But we had some direct fund-raising weapons of our own. One of them was called "George V. Cooper."

Quick story. George Cooper, a member of the Citizens Finance Committee, had spent a fair amount of time working with Eisenhower when Ike was at Columbia. George was active in the Alumni Association, and Ike asked him to help with two projects—to reorganize the Association, and to help him promote the new American Assembly, a non-partisan Eisenhower initiative to bring great minds together to study the problems facing the nation (it is still active, today). George and Ike traveled together through much of the country, riding in a private rail car attached to whatever train was headed where they wanted to go. George got to know Ike, very well.

Skip ahead a couple of years . . . in the buildup to the Republican National Convention, George was a major fundraiser for Citizens, simply telling audiences along the Atlantic coast and in the Midwest, what he knew about Eisenhower as a man, not as a war hero or politician. I believe he raised several million dollars. Then, after the convention, he went back on the road and raised about the same amount of money, especially in support of the television effort. [56]

He made it seem easy although I know he had some problems with local and state Republican leaders because they thought we—meaning, "Citizens"—were intercepting contributions that would have, should have, gone to the Party. Well, George was not the only Citizens fundraiser to be the target of such criticism, but in our defense I can truthfully say that a large portion of our funds came from Independents and Democrats, folks who might have been reluctant to make a contribution to the Republican Party. And —point of order—the money was going to support the candidacy of Dwight Eisenhower and it should have made little difference to anyone through which door it had gained entry.

Now, I have been describing the TV spot campaign in which we—"Citizens," and especially Charlie and me—had been directly involved from the start. There was one other spot, not connected with any advertising agency, which we didn't know about until Jackie Cochrane brought it from Hollywood and showed it to our team in her New York City apartment. And it has a story all its own. [57] Jackie was responsible for the creation of a campaign spot ranked as one of the ten-best, ever, by *Time* magazine.

Jackie was a tireless traveler on behalf of Ike. At first, she was invited to ride the Campaign train, but she found that to be a waste of her time; she was much more effective out on the stump, flying her own plane to parts of the nation where the commercial airlines were rather sparse, giving speeches to women's groups.

She was affiliated with an Eisenhower support group in her home state of California, which wanted to produce a spot for local distribution that would show Democrats slaughtering baby pigs and otherwise being involved in questionable behavior reflecting protectionist activities during the Depression. Jackie was appalled. She told the group that they needed something upbeat, that could be seen by the whole family—"In other words, a Disney."

As it happened, Jackie's husband, Floyd Odlum, was a director of the Disney Corporation, and soon enough Walt Disney and his brother Roy were directly involved. There was one issue to be resolved: Disney was a union shop, and the work rules prohibited any partisan political activity. But if the work could be done by unpaid volunteers working outside of normal working hours? No problem.

As for a theme . . . a Disney staff nurse wrote out a little ditty, "You like Ike, I like Ike, everybody likes Ike" which, set to music, became the core of the spot that was produced by Roy Disney, himself.

The "characters" included the proverbial butcher, baker, and candlestick maker—along with a fireman, a

policeman, a housewife, a farmer, a cowboy—images representing a range of professions marching in step to the perky choral soundtrack, along with a jaunty Uncle Sam and a baby elephant beating the drum for Eisenhower.

Disney called the one-minute spot "We'll Take Ike" — as in, "We'll take Ike to Washington." But for obvious reasons, it has always been known as, "I Like Ike." In part:

> Ike for President, Ike for President, Ike for President, Ike for President . . .You like Ike, I like Ike, ev'ry body likes Ike for President . . . hang out the banners beat the drums we'll take Ike to Washington . . . get in step with the man who's hep, get in step with Ike. [58]

It was the only Eisenhower spot that took a swipe, however gentle, at Stevenson—who was not even mentioned in the Rosser Reeves spots. As the troop of Eisenhower supporters marched from left to right—the direction indicated by a road sign pointing to the "White House"—the silhouette of a donkey with a rider was in the background, moving in the other direction while the singers intoned, "We got to get where we are going, travel day and night, let Adlai go the other way we'll all go with Ike."

The Disney services were all gratis—volunteers, not the company, created the spot—and Jackie donated some $2700 to pay for more than four hundred prints of the one-minute (and an edited twenty-second version) which were shipped to major television stations throughout the country. For our part, we "sponsored" the Disney spot and assembled a "kit" of the Reeves TV and radio spots, which we promoted to all of our local Ike clubs ("Now available! All the issues met fairly and squarely!"). Our goal was to have at least five or six spots a night in targeted areas, over the last two weeks before the election.

Success? I cannot score the campaign, there were too many issues, too many variables, and to this day I don't think anyone can truly gauge the impact of TV spots on any Presidential campaign. In 1952, our 31 spots were aired in at least 40 states and Eisenhower lost only one of those states, Kentucky. Overall cost? Unknown, because so much of the time was purchased by local and state groups. I have no idea how many were used, or how many times they were shown, but I do know that, at one point, the spots were saturating the New York City market, TV and radio, at a rate of about 140 a day. Which by itself probably cost about $1 million. And . . . we won New York.

As footnote, of sorts, call it, our own head-to-head competition, the Disney folks later told Ms. Cochran that "we have been advised by the stations that these cartoon spots were played more than any of the other Eisenhower television films." [59] *Time* magazine ranked the "upbeat and cute" Disney spot as number 8 in a list of the top 10 campaign ads of all time. [60] It is in good company; let me mention two of which I'm sure you are aware.

Number 1 on the list is the 1964 LBJ ad "Daisy

Girl," where a little girl plucks a daisy while a doomsday voice counts down to a nuclear explosion.

Number 5: Hillary Clinton's 2008 primary campaign ad,

> "It's 3 A.M. . . . there's a phone in the White House, and it's ringing . . . something's happening in the world . . . your vote will determine who answers that call . . ."

That, by the way, was a 30-second spot. The spirit of Rosser Reeves, is with us yet.

The executive director of "Volunteers for Stevenson," George W. Ball, charged that our spots had been conceived by "high powered hucksters of Madison Avenue" and that they were trying to "sell Eisenhower to voters in the same manner as soap, ammoniated toothpaste, hair tonic or bubblegum." Stevenson himself told an audience in Cincinnati, October 3, "I don't think the American people want politics and the presidency to become the plaything of the high-pressure men, of the ghost writers, or the public-relations men." [61] He told a CBS reporter, "This is the worst thing I've ever heard of, selling the presidency like cereal. How can you talk seriously about issues with half minute spots?" [62] The Democrats tried to get the Federal Communications Commission (FCC) to stop the campaign—they charged that the Republicans were violating the equal time provision of the communication act of 1934 and/or the provisions of the corrupt practices act to create some sort of broadcast monopoly. Monopoly? Just one example: a Stevenson group learned that the Republicans planned to run 1300 spots on 11 radio and three television stations in Philadelphia between October 14 and election day. The head of the Senate Interstate and Foreign Commerce Committee (Sen. Edwin Johnson, D-Colorado) charged that, nationwide, the spot campaign "appears designed to monopolize the airways for GOP propaganda during the closing days of the 1952 campaign," which would be "in direct conflict with the spirit, if not the letter of the law." [63]

The FCC refused to act, because they saw nothing illegal in our effort, we were renting air time just as anyone might do. So, the Democrats began running spots of their own; they weren't very numerous, nor very good:

> It's Adlai to you, Adlee to me, I don't care how you quote it / Adlee Adlai. . . don't pronounce it, just go out and vote it! / STEVENSON. [64]

The Dems effort was tardy, because they didn't have the money to pay for the program. George Ball said, "We are broke because unlike our Republican opponents we do not have great banks and investment houses, the steel masters and oil magnates, the motor makers, the money makers to underwrite our campaign." However, he admitted, they now were trying to raise money to "counter sham with truth."

To the best of my knowledge, they spent only about $77,000 on their effort—total. And Governor Stevenson himself refused to participate. It may have been a cultural thing. TV was new, TV was, well, kind of lower class. As noted by journalist David Halberstam, people in Stevenson's circle "refused to admit they even watched television, let alone owned one." [65]

However, both parties were using paid television to carry non-newsworthy campaign events and speeches. The Democrats booked 18 30-minute timeslots well in advance. The RNC, on the other hand, preempted top shows at the last minute, paying the extra costs in hopes of maintaining the audience that had tuned in to watch, for example, the *Arthur Godfrey Show*. I'm not sure what was, or was not, more effective. Clearly, the viewers would have to be interested in the candidate in the first place or they wouldn't bother to watch an announced program. And viewers who were surprised to discover that they had been kicked-off "Godfrey" might well have harbored some resentment.

CHAPTER THIRTEEN

As the campaign was winding down we organized a "hard hitting" letter writing campaign to "tell the Eisenhower story in language every voter can understand." Four letters, to be mailed in the three weeks just before the election.

The letters were signed by Walter Williams, "National Chairman, Citizens for Eisenhower-Nixon," and each began with an attention grabbing headline:

Will you vote to continue coddling the Russians?

Will you vote for higher living costs for your family?

Will you vote to have more of your money stolen by the corrupt gang in Washington?

How you can become the most important person in the world…

As the opening lines of this last letter explained:

Dear VOTER: On November 4—by pulling a lever on a little machine, or putting a little mark like this (X) on a piece of paper—you can become the most important person in the world why? Because…

On that November day you can elect the man who is to determine the course of America for the next four years! You know his name—Dwight D. Eisenhower!

Our strategy: to enlist the aid of prominent businessman around the country, to send these letters to their friends, relatives, and employees—at minimal out-of-pocket cost. We would supply 250 sets of the four letters, including envelopes, for $30; they would have someone address and mail the letters, affixing first-class postage (three cents). For the more cost-conscious among them we pointed out, "if you do not seal the flaps, the letters will go as second-class mail and require only two cents postage each." (We also cautioned, that since corporations could not legally make political contributions, this mailing must be an individual, not company, effort.)

Election eve was host to dueling television. It started with a Republican program (broadcast at the same time on both ABC and NBC) that was carried on 50 stations and reached more than 6 million viewers. This was followed by several Stevenson programs featuring speeches by supporters that reached 7.5 million people over 89 stations. The evening ended with a one-hour Eisenhower program on 83 stations that reached 7.3 million people. And then, at midnight, the voting began.

Election Day, November 4, 1952. We knew that we had more than 1 million volunteers (Walter Williams estimated 2.5 million)[66] beating the bushes to get folks headed for the polls. And, it was a record turnout, nearly 13,000,000 more voters than in 1948, and it was an electoral landslide for Eisenhower. He scored 55 percent of the popular vote and 442 of the 531 electoral votes. The nine states he didn't carry were all in the East-of-the-Mississippi-River Deep South, but in that region, he won Virginia, Tennessee, and Florida. And, while he didn't win Alabama, the *Montgomery Advertiser*—for the first time in its 124-year history—had endorsed a Republican. Ike's "Southern Strategy" was not wasted.

Another record of sorts: "Citizens" had money left over. Treasurer Sidney Weinberg had, right at the start, laid down some basic rules. No donor money was to be used for chauffeured limousines, high-priced hotels, and fancy dinners. All expenditures were to be strictly accounted. This did lead to some issues: Citizens was spending perhaps $1000 a day in what politicians would call "walking around money." Tips to the cops who maintained order, five dollars apiece. Payments to the union band members who marched in the parades. While Sidney's rules required receipts, "walking around money" did not generate any, and the staffers passing out the dollars were, for a time, left holding the bag until Sidney took a close look and said, in essence, he trusted the workers and approved the payments.

At the end, even after all lingering expenses had

been paid and storage arranged for the files, there was money in the till. Sidney pro-rated the surplus and sent it back to our contributors.

Soon after the election, Eisenhower invited me and Charlie over to his headquarters at the Commodore Hotel, where, with a broad smile, he said, "You two SOBs are responsible for me being here! I want you to come with me to Washington, any job you want." Well, perhaps a bit of hyperbole, he didn't mean I could be Secretary of Commerce . . . but I did take a job as special assistant to the Under Secretary of Commerce (which, in 1953, was the number two man in the department).

Soon enough, I saw an opportunity to make a significant contribution. Members of the administration were eager to go on the stump and extol the policies of the government . . . except, most of them didn't really know what those policies might be. There were 1200 political appointees crisscrossing the country without guidance or coordination. So, with the support of the President, I created the Executive Branch Liaison Office, which had two principal functions: to develop and distribute weekly Fact Sheets, and to coordinate public appearances, spreading the wealth, so to speak.

The Fact Sheets presented up-to-date comments and statements by the President and Cabinet Officers, and explained administration programs and accomplishments. The "coordination" was inspired when I found, for example, six appointees making presentations at one conference, but none showing up at another, equally-important, event. So we imposed a requirement, advance clearance for all speeches—not for content, but for venue, to ensure equal opportunity for all appropriate audiences to enjoy representation from the Administration.

Charlie went into the White House as assistant to the new Chief of Staff, Sherman Adams, where he was in charge of the Personnel Management Program (call it, political appointments and patronage). Charlie established procedures for identifying vacancies of Schedule C positions and all positions at the level of GS-14 and above, and for soliciting recommendations for replacement candidates from members of the Congress and Republican Party leaders. To the best of my knowledge, some of his practices are still in use today. He left in July, 1955, and, having long since sold his interest in Willis-Rose, took a civilian job that he discovered he didn't like . . . assistant to the chairman of W. R. Grace Company. He didn't like it, because there wasn't much to do, so he became the CEO of Alaskan Airlines. And took it from near-death to great success.

Other staffers who went into the Administration? Practically everyone with whom we had worked. Mary Lord became U.S. representative to the United Nations Human Rights Commission and also served as U. S. delegate to the United Nations General

Assembly. Walter Williams served as Undersecretary of Commerce 1953-1958—where he was my boss for a time; Jock Whitney went to England as our Ambassador (a position once held by his grandfather, John Hay); Gabriel Hauge served as assistant to the President for Economic Affairs, 1953-58, and, later, became a Director of the Council on Foreign Relations and Chairman of Manufacturers Hanover Trust. Abbott Washburn was involved in the creation, and became Deputy Director of, the U.S. Information Agency (USIA). Our travel coordinator, D. Walter Swan, became Deputy Assistant Secretary of Defense for Public Affairs 1953-54.

Bob Mullen went with Paul Hoffman to the Ford Foundation and was involved in the creation of Citizens for Educational Television (soon to be known as the Corporation for Public Broadcasting); Bob Mullen's assistant at Citizens for Eisenhower, Gil Robinson, became the first employee. (Later, in the Reagan Administration, Gil served as deputy director at USIA and as special advisor to the Secretary of State with the rank of ambassador). Another Mullen assistant, Jack Beardwood (press relations), became executive assistant to Oveta Culp Hobby, she was the first Secretary of Health, Education, and Welfare. Lodge, who lost his senate re-election bid to John F. Kennedy, became Ambassador to the United Nations.

By December, 1955, I was ready to move along. The President asked me to stay on, perhaps to serve as ambassador to some nation where my lack of diplomatic experience would not be a handicap. In other words—no offense—some nation that was not a leader on the world stage. I was flattered, but, frankly, I knew I would not be happy in a job where—no offense—each morning was spent reading the daily guidance from the State Department. I did take a two-year appointment as Chairman of the U. S. Committee for the United Nations, in New York City. Our mission: working with a number of major businesses and professional groups, to raise money and cultivate support for the United Nations.

Deenie, after having three children, was moving ahead with her show business career. She had done a few bits on Broadway, some television, and in 1957 had her first movie role, working with Spencer Tracy and Katherine Hepburn in "Desk Set."

My appointment to the Committee worked out well, because I was free to do what I believe I did best—create and nurture new businesses. Here's one example, of some 40 that I set up, over the years. Someone told me that the citizens of Trinidad had to import flour from the United Sates—at great expense and with much of it, in 100-pound sacks, at risk of damage from the shipping and the heat. An opportunity? I met with the Prime Minister, he helped me get some property on the harbor, where I built the Trinidad Flour Mills—some silos to store wheat and a mill to grind it on demand, at far lower cost than importing the finished product.

One day, I was playing golf with George Pillsbury, a friend from our days together at Yale . . . he said, "I understand you have built a flour mill in Trinidad, could I bring my company [Pillsbury] in as an investor?" I said certainly, and asked him, why had no one done this before? He told me about an unwritten agreement among U. S. companies, they would discourage any efforts to create an indigenous flour-producing industry and thus preserve the Caribbean as an export market. Well, I clearly (albeit unwittingly) had broken up that monopoly. George's investment was good business for both of us, not just in Trinidad but we soon opened a Flour and Feed Mill in Jamaica.

Once the election was past, Charlie and I were no longer involved—we had achieved our goals—but Citizens for Eisenhower remained in business, in somewhat compromised fashion. Yes, Citizens played a role in 1954 (with Gil Robinson filling in as PR director, working on 30 congressional campaigns) and for the Presidential campaign of 1956—the Bandwagons were expanded to six units, every bit as effective as before. Lang Washburn, who had gone back to his job at Hiller Helicopters after the election, became involved in planning for the 1956 Republican National Convention and then served as director of campaign activities for the Bandwagon Operation. (He did finally enter government service, Assistant Secretary of Commerce for Tourism, 1970-1975.)

But . . . there were changes that impeded, in my

judgment, success. For example—by 1956—all top officers were being paid. In my opinion, then and still today, it is impossible to have a truly volunteer organization if the leadership is being paid. A certain feeling of resentment and greed takes hold, and the volunteers often feel that they are tools to be used, and not equal partners.

Well, I leave that for others to judge. For now, I am proud of our effort, and humbled that it seems to have made a difference.

EPILOG:
A LOOK BACK, AND AHEAD

Ambassador Gilbert A. Robinson (Ret)

A few years ago, I assembled the 30 "Why I Like Ike" newspaper columns I had written back in 1952, added some new material, and issued a small book to ensure that the stories would survive for at least a few more years. One of the additions was a brief description of "Citizens for Eisenhower," contributed by my friend, Stanley Rumbough.

Yes, I had been involved in "Citizens," but I was, at the time, a very junior member of the team, focused on getting out press releases. Stanley's addition to my book told me more about his efforts on behalf of Eisenhower than I had known at the time, about the origin of the movement, about his partner Charlie Willis, and about some of the unorthodox methods they undertook to reach their goals (to get Ike to say "yes," to get him the nomination, and to help him win the election).

It was easy to see that so much more could be written about "Citizens," with a view toward influencing a future "Citizens-for-Someone" campaign effort. Since I had recently taken over a small publishing company (International Publishers), I suggested that Stanley write a book, and-in his typically low-key manner- he said, "Why not?"

Brayton Harris, my executive editor, embarked on a six-month-long series of recorded conversations with Stanley, which form the basis of this narrative. I added some useful information and illustrations from Stanley's scrapbooks and my own files, Stanley pulled everything together, and you are holding the result in your hands.

I thought we might end up with an interesting moment in political history. We got that, but so much more, on two counts. First, the book is also a fascinating look at the entrepreneurial success (and government-abetted failure) of two young war heroes who wanted to start an airline, and, second, it is a primer, a template, a road map for a future presidential campaign . . . in particular, one that may not be dependent on the existing Republican or Democrat organizations.

In 1952, "Citizens" proved the value of working with voters who were not affiliated with either party; at the time, about 15 percent identified themselves as "Independent." Today, according to a January, 2012 Gallup Poll, about 40 percent of all voters say they are Independent! [67] More than Democrats (31 percent) and Republicans (27 percent).

There have been other changes in the political and social landscape since 1952, some of which will certainly be at play in elections of the future. For example, you can sign up a million "friends" on Facebook in a very short time or establish a presence on Twitter and other social media and collect comments from thousands of people in a matter of minutes.

The challenge is to convert those correspondents into active members of your club, your movement, your campaign. A "list of friends" does not translate into action.

Stan and Charlie built their "Eisenhower for President Clubs" the old-fashioned way, one leader, one member, one step at a time. They organized a team of committed volunteers, along with fund-raisers, attorneys, public relations experts, and advertising gurus—all working on behalf of a charismatic and well-grounded candidate. They not only created an organization that helped recruit and elect President Eisenhower, but designed a model that could be used today by any Republican, Democrat . . . or Independent . . . candidate for President of the United States.

NOTES & SOURCES
To aid the curious reader or energetic researcher

Back cover: Eisenhower quote, reported in Willis, Charles F., Columbia University Oral History Project, interview by John T. Mason, Jr., March 15, 1968. OH-86. 12.

1 The record of Willis Air Service—and the actions of the CAB—are fully-explored in "Hearings before the Committee on Interstate and Foreign Commerce, United States Senate: Air-line Industry Investigation, Part I and Part II, 81st Congress, 1st Session." (1949).

2 *NYTimes*, July 16, 1949.

3 Kelly, Charles J. *Tex McCrary: Wars-Women-Politics; An Adventurous Life Across the American Century* (Hamilton Books, Lanham, MD, 2009) 129.

4 Some years ago, I donated several copies of the "Handbook" to the Eisenhower Presidential Library, where—along with other of my papers —they are now available for study, filed in Rumbough, Stanley M. Jr.: Papers 1952-57, Accession 00-5, Box 1

5 *NYTimes*, Jan 25 1948.

6 Dick, Jane. *Volunteers and the Making of Presidents.*(Dodd, Mead and Company, 1980) 78.

7 All, cited in the *NYTimes*, Dec 2, 1951.

8 Eisenhower, Dwight D. *Mandate for Change* (Doubleday and Company, Inc. Garden City, New York, 1963) 17.

9 *Ibid*, 19.

10 *NYTimes*, Dec. 2, 1951.

11 Eisenhower, *op. cit.* 19; Ambrose, Stephen E. *Eisenhower: Soldier and President* (A Touchstone Book. New York, 1990) 259-260.

12 *NYTimes*, Dec 4, 1951.

13 Adams, Sherman; *First Hand Report: The Story of the Eisenhower Administration* (New York: Harper and Brothers, 1961). 13.

14 *NYTimes*, Jan 7, 1952.

15 Adams, op. cit. 20.

16 *NYTimes* Jan 27, 1952.

17 *TIME*, Jan 28, 1952.

18 Ambrose, *op. cit.* 264.

19 Kelly, *op. cit.* 132.

20 Eisenhower, *op. cit.* 20.

21 Cochrane, Jacqueline. Eisenhower Library Oral History Project, interview by John E. Wickman. (OH-42) Interview #1, (1968). Her Madison Square Garden story, 13-33.

22 Dick, *op. cit.* 96.

23 Michael J. Birkner, "The 'Draft Eisenhower' Movement." *Historical New Hampshire*, Vol 58 Nos 1 & 2, Spring-Summer 2003; 12.

24 Oles, Floyd. Dwight D. Eisenhower Library Oral History Project, interview by Maclyn Burg, 1972, (OH-249) 20-21.

25 Eisenhower, *op. cit.* 35.

26 *Ibid*, n. 22.

27 Kelly, *op. cit.* 138.

28 *NYTimes*, April 3, 1952.

29 Pickett, William B. *Eisenhower Decides to Run* (Ivan R. Dee, Chicago, 2000) 204.

30 Washburn, Abbott. Columbia University Oral History Project, interview #1, by Ed Edwin, April 20, 1967 (OH-124), 28.

31 http://en.wikipedia.org/wiki/Republican_party_presidential_primaries_1952

32 Eisenhower, *op. cit.* 34.

33 Benedict, Stephen H. Columbia University Oral History Project, interview by Herbert Parmet, April 9, 1969; Part II. 34.

34 Eisenhower, *op. cit.* 35.

35 Ambrose, *op. cit.* 270.

36 Zaghi, Frederick. Eisenhower Library Oral History Project, interview by Dr. John E. Wickman, 1968 (OH-107). 1-7.

37 Nixon's candidacy almost ended before the campaign began; he soon came under public scrutiny for what some folks thought was acceptance of an illegal slush fund. It was not, but was controversial enough that he

went on television to explain. . . and to defend his acceptance, on behalf of his daughters, of the gift of a cocker spaniel named "Checkers."

38 Young & Rubicam undated memo "The Eisenhower campaign: a copy policy." Eisenhower Library, Young and Rubicam, Inc.: Records of Citizens for Eisenhower 1952-1961, Box 1

39 Thayer, Walter. Columbia University Oral History Project, interview by John Luter, 1967 (OH 272) 7.

40 Washburn, *op. cit.* 18

41 *LIFE*, Oct 6, 1952.

42 www.thebluereview.org/red-tide-rising/ Retrieved July 1, 2013.

43 *LIFE*, Oct 6, 1952.

44 Flyer announcing rally; Eisenhower Library, Washburn, C. Langhorne: Papers, Box 2.

45 *LIFE*, Oct 6, 1952.

46 Eisenhower, *op. cit.* 58.

47 Swan, Walter. Eisenhower Library Oral History Project, interview by Maclyn P. Burg and Thomas F. Soapes, 1976. Discussion of travel arrangements and conditions, 11-49.

48 Benedict, Stephen H. *op. cit.* Diary entry for Sept. 22, 1952.

49 *NYTimes*, Oct 2, 1952.

50 Gordon Cotler, "That Plague of Spots From Madison Avenue" *The Reporter* November 25, 1952.

51 Halberstam, David. *The Fifties* (The Random House Publishing Group, New York. 1993) 232.

52 *Ibid* 230.

53 http://www.livingroomcandidate.org/commercials/1952/never-had-it-so-good. Retrieved July 1, 2013.

54 "Spots for Eisenhower," booklet produced by Rosser Reeves. Copy in Eisenhower Library, Rumbough, Stanley M. Jr.: Papers 1952-57, Accession 00-5, Box 1.

55 Petersen, Howard. Columbia University Oral History Project, interview by John T. Mason, Jr., 1968,

56 Cooper, George V. Eisenhower Library Oral History Project. 1, 14.

57 The "Disney" story is well told in Cochran, *op. cit.* 47-55

58 http://www.livingroomcandidate.org/commercials/1952/never-had-it-so-good. Retrieved July 1, 2013.

59 Personal Letter, Bill Anderson to Cochran, November 19, 1952. Eisenhower Library, Jacqueline Cochran: Papers, Eisenhower Campaign Series, Box 2.

60 http://www.time.com/time/specials/ packages/Completelist/0.29569, 1842516,00.html. Retrieved 1 August 2013.

61 *NYTimes*, Oct 4, 1952.

62 Halberstam, *op. cit.* 232.

63 *Presidential Studies Quarterly* vol 20 no 2; Eisenhower centennial issue spring 1990. 265-283.

64 http://www.livingroomcandidate.org/commercials/1952/never-had-it-so-good Retrieved July 1, 2013.

65 John E. Hollitz, "Eisenhower and the Admen: The Television "Spot" Campaign of 1952." *Wisconsin Magazine of History*, Vol 66 No 1, Autumn 1982. *Also*, Halberstam, *op. cit.* 232.

66 Williams, W. Walter. Columbia University Oral History Project, interview by John T. Mason, Jr., Part I, OH-276. 20

67 http://www.gallup.com/poll/151943/record-high-americans-identify-independents.aspx retrieved July 27, 2013.

"CITIZENS FOR EISENHOWER" SOURCES

The following items were of great assistance is refreshing my memory and filling in some blanks; all are available at the Eisenhower Presidential Library in Abilene, KS, and some of the Oral Histories can be viewed on-line.

To see summaries of document holdings, visit
http://www.eisenhower.archives.gov/research/finding_aids.html

To view the full Oral History collection:
http://www.eisenhower.archives.gov/research/oral_histories.html

ORAL HISTORIES

Benedict, Stephen H. Columbia University Oral History, interviews by John T. Mason, Jr., Sept. 13, 1968, Oct. 18, 1969, Dec. 6, 1968, OH-210. 137 pages.

Cochran, Jacqueline, Eisenhower Library Oral History Project, OH-42, interview by John E. Wickman, 1968.

Cooper, George V. Eisenhower Library Oral History Project, OH-393, 35 pages.

Gray, Arthur, Jr. Columbia University Oral History Project, interview by John Luter, 1968, OH-55. 33 pages.

Greunther, Homer. Columbia University Oral History Project, interview by John T. Mason, Jr., 1972, OH-254. 108 pages.

Hauge, Gabriel. Columbia University Oral History Project Interviews, 1967, OH-190. 132 pages.

Petersen, Howard C. Columbia University Oral History Project, interview by John T. Mason, Jr., 1968, OH-227. 70 pages.

Rumbough, Stanley M. Jr. Columbia University Oral History Project, interview by John T. Mason, Jr., 1967, OH-68. 40 pages.

Swan, D. Walter. . Eisenhower Library Oral History Project, OH-343, interview by Maclyn P. Burg and Thomas F. Soapes, 1976. 95 pages.

Thayer, Walter N. Columbia University Oral History Project, interview by John Luter, 1967, OH-272. 53 pages.

Washburn, Mr. And Mrs. Abbott. Columbia University Oral History Project, interview by Ed Edwin, January 5, 1968, OH-124 91 pages.

Williams, W. Walter Columbia University Oral History Project, interview by John T. Mason, Jr., Part I, September 20, 1967. OH-276 104 pages

Willis, Charles F. Jr. Columbia University Oral History Project interview by John T. Mason, Jr., March 15, 1968. OH-86. 51 pages.

OTHER PERTINENT RECORDS

Brownell, Herbert: Papers, Box 126.

Jacqueline Cochran: Papers, Eisenhower Campaign Series, Box 2.

Rumbough, Stanley M. Jr.: Papers 1952-57, Accession 00-5, Box 1 .

Washburn, C. Langhorne: Papers, Box 1, Box 2, Box 3, Box 15.

Young and Rubicam, Inc.: Records of Citizens for Eisenhower 1952-1961, Box 1.

INDEX

Trinidad Flour Mills, 121

Truman, President Harry S 17, 19, 34-35, 45, 50, 72, 83, 102

"Offers" Presidency to Ike, 1945, 26

Repeats offer, 1951, 34

Typical campaign swing, 93

"Unique Selling Proposition", 99

U.S. Committee for the United Nations, 121

Vandenberg, Arthur, Jr., 37-38

Vermont, 85

Veterans of Foreign Wars (VFW), 76-77

Volunteers for Stevenson, 112

Waco, 93

"Walking around money," 117

Waring, Fred, 54

Warren, Governor Earl, 59

Washburn, Langhorne (Special events), 21, 54, 58-59, 66, 75, 80, 82, 120, 122

"We Love the Sunshine of Your Smile", 79

Weinberg, Sidney ("Citizens" treasurer), 38, 96, 117

West Point, 5

West Virginia, 55

Whistle-stops, 89-90

Whitney, John Hay "Jock" (Fundraiser), 38, 47, 51, 87, 95-96, 105, 120

"Why I Like Ike" (newspaper series), 41

Williams, W. Walter (Co-chairman), 38, 41, 73, 86, 96, 115, 117, 120

Willis Air Service, 10-16

Willis, Charles F., Jr.

Post-election jobs, 119

Service in World War II, 10

Willis, Grace "Bo," 8, 9

Willis-Rose Corporation, 15

Willkie, Wendell (Presidential candidate, 1940), 17, 33

Yale University, 5, 8, 56, 122

"You never had it so good!" (Democrat campaign slogan), 95

Young & Rubicam develops print advertising campaign, 72

Young Industry for Eisenhower (YIFE), 21, 31, 42, 58, 66, 74

Young Presidents Organization, 20

Youth for Eisenhower, 31, 38, 42

Zaghi, Frederick A. (Y&R Advertising Agency), 55, 69